Your Walk,
their walk

A Field Guide for Leading Your Children
in the *Word of God*

J. MICHAEL CUNNINGHAM

Your Walk, Their Walk:
A Field Guide for Leading Your Children in the Word of God
ISBN: 978-0-88144-111-6
Copyright © 2010 by Mike Cunningham

Published by
Thorncrown Publishing
9731 East 54th Street
Tulsa, OK 74146
www.thorncrownpublishing.com

CONTENTS

ACKNOWLEDGEMENTS

Acknowledgements in books have always seemed a way for authors to sort of give a passing mention to some of their friends. The words of thanks, while seeming sincere, appeared to be just a required afterthought to fill one of the tasks needed to complete a book.

I have discovered that this assumption could not be more wrong.

I have come to understand that while my name may be on the cover, it would not have gotten there without the support and encouragement of many people. Not even close. So while my name may be on the cover, this is as much their book as it is mine.

My wife of nearly 32 years, Jenny, has encouraged me and put up with my not being available as I have put this together. She is a perfect complement to my gifts and abilities. I cannot imagine living life without her. She contributed her knowledge of children with special needs by reviewing and critiquing that portion of Chapter Seven.

My daughter Ranae sometimes wonders if people know that I have a daughter since I spend so much time talking about fathers investing in their sons. So let me brag for a moment. She is beautiful and multi-talented. Her capacity for people is unmatched. Though we focus on sons in our workshops, a lot of what we share was shaped by our experiences with Ranae.

My sons, John, Jeff, and Brian, have attended the workshops for the past two years and shared with the men what they have learned. The evaluations we receive are unanimous. The involvement of my sons validates what we teach in our workshops, and it gives fathers who attend hope that they can do this with their kids.

If it were not for Dave Jewitt's prodding, our ministry Entrusting Truth, and thus, this book would not be.

I am indebted to many men who showed me how to study the Bible. Harry Steck started me on verse analysis, and Terry Cook shared what he had learned about synthetic Bible study. Chuck Steen taught me by example to continue in the Word for life, Larry Whitehouse equipped me to build my ministry on the Word, and John Hamilton continues to push me with difficult questions. Lastly, in the place of honor, I thank Dr. Howard Hendricks, whose eight tape series on synthetic Bible study led me to dig deeper than I knew I could. I obtained the notes from his course on Advanced Bible Study at Dallas Seminary from one of his graduates. I used those notes and tapes to craft much of what I taught others to do in Bible Study for years. Thirty-one years later, my son John found those same messages in MP3 form on a website. After listening to them several times, he called and wanted me to teach him the method.

Kip Karney and Kim Hand read several of the chapters and gave critical feedback. Gary Barkalow, Dave Jewitt, and John Hamilton read the first chapter and added their thoughts. Joe Scruggs Ph.D, clinical psychologist and interim pastor of my church, read the difficult sections on children of divorce and blended families and gave valuable feedback and insight.

Dan and Nancy Roberts, Redeemer Covenant Church, Brian and Donna Flesner, Al and Stephanie Howerton, Gary and Leigh Barkalow, Chris Bourne, Brent Lollis, Bob Skaggs, Clark

Milspaugh, Brian Phillips, Buck and Joy Strickland, John and Jeannie Hamilton, Perry and Becky Clark, Clinton Godwin, Mike King, Lance and Mary Jo Smith, Jeff and Kara Shaw, Bob and Sabrina Triplett, Don McDonald, and Jeff and Judy Davis have at different times supported the fledgling ministry of Entrusting Truth. If it were not for their belief and support of what we are doing, we would not be doing it.

John A. Cunningham is my dad. He is one of my heroes and his support of this book and our ministry means more than can be expressed in words. Thank you, Dad.

INTRODUCTION

I do not have all of this figured out. As you read this book, you may think we have this child-training thing nailed. Nope. We are in process just as you are. I have had the privilege of interacting with a lot of men over the past two years on this topic and have learned much from these interactions. As I was writing this book, I realized some of this we have done well. But there were things I wish I had tried or done better. The bottom line is that there is no magic formula. As evangelicals, we lean heavily on Proverbs 22:6: "Train up a child in the way he should go, even when he is old he will not depart from it." But reality is that Proverbs is not a guide to human spiritual behavior. It is a book of how life can generally be lived well. Proverbs 22:6 is not a promise, but it is a generally true principle of life. As with any principle, there are exceptions.

My wife and I have good friends who, unable to get pregnant, have endured the adoption process twice. Several years ago, the husband and I spent a weekend away in a cabin, weeping over one of his children. Though this child was exposed to much of what we will cover in these pages, this child chose to rebel, drifting away from their faith and their family into illegal activities. My friend had to have this child arrested by the authorities while sitting together at the kitchen table. Yet, their other child responded positively to the same home and training, and that child is walking with God.

We are completely dependent on the Lord for our children. We cannot force them to walk with God. All we can do is pray and trust in His mercy and grace.

If you picked up this book hoping to find the sure-fire solution to having your children walk with God, you should put it back down. But, if you are looking for some ideas to help you expose your children more consistently to the Word of God — keep reading.

The basic premise of this book is that if you are going to lead your children in the Word of God, you are going to have to commit to studying it for yourself, regardless of their response. In other words, you have to be sold out to walking with God. You then invite them to join with you in the process.

So, to reverse Rick Warren's opening sentence, it is about you.

The first three chapters lay a foundation for why and how we should be going after our kids' hearts. Chapters Four and Five lay the groundwork for what you can do in the Word with your children, along with ideas on how to encourage them to be involved in the process.

Chapter Six suggests some pitfalls to avoid. And if you are facing the challenge of having children dealing with your divorce, children in a blended family, or a child with special needs, Chapter Seven may prove to be of some help.

When I worked with the Charles E. Fuller Institute of Evangelism and Church Growth, we spent the last day of a four-day workshop on church growth talking about and helping church teams plan to implement the information we had shared with them during the week. Part of those exercises was the acknowledgement that there would be challenges ahead as they applied what they had learned. This will be no different. We will cover that in more detail along with some strategies to overcome any resistance in chapter Eight.

In the workshops we hold for men, one or more of my sons come in for the last thirty minutes so the audience can ask them questions about what we have done together. I have learned a lot listening to them. In Chapter Ten I have pulled some of the questions off of the recordings of the workshops along with my sons' responses.

You will get the most out of this book if you attempt to do the studies outlined in Chapter Four. To help you there is a companion workbook that walks you through the studies and gives you a point of comparison. I would recommend that you work through it with your son or daughter and/or with a group of men who are also committed to this journey.

The focus here is obviously for fathers to spiritually train and teach their children. However, this works with spiritual children as well. These studies and this approach will also succeed with men you have led to the Lord and are helping walk as an apprentice of Jesus.

There is more to being an apprentice of Christ than Bible study. Much more. But one of the foundational pillars is consistent time alone with God in His Word. The other disciplines are outside the scope of this book. I have found that engaging in this one discipline, at least for me and for many that I know, leads to engaging in the others. I pray that will be your experience as well.

I am passionate about this. I hope that communicates. I am praying that you will find the process engaging and you and your children will be drawn through the Word into the richness that is our Lord.

Mike Cunningham
Tulsa, 2010

For Mom who dreamed it.

CHAPTER 1
Fighting for Our Kids

I love the movie *Taken;* well, love may be too strong. After viewing it, I could not sleep. I have a daughter and the thought that something like that could happen to her was just about more than I could stand. In the movie, actor Liam Neeson's character, Bryan Mills, is a retired government agent. Against his wishes, his estranged daughter travels to France with her friend to follow U2 on tour. Shortly after getting to their room, four men show up and kidnap them. Bryan's daughter, Kim, is on the phone with him when the men show up. Bryan immediately walks her through what to do to give him the information he needs to try to find her. After she is taken, one of her captors picks up her cell phone. Bryan says to him, "I don't know who you are. I don't know what you want. If you are looking for ransom, I can tell you I don't have money. But what I do have are a very particular set of skills, skills I have acquired over a very long career. Skills that make me a nightmare for people like you. If you let my daughter go now, that'll be the end of it. I will not look for you; I will not pursue you. But if you don't, I will look for you; I will find you, and I will kill you."[1]

---

[1] *Taken.* Director Pierre Morel, Twentieth Century Fox, EropaCorp, M6 Films, and Grive Productions. Beverly Hills, CA: Twentieth Century Fox Home Entertainment, 2009, DVD recording.

If you are familiar with this movie, you know that from this point Bryan uses his "very particular set of skills" to rescue his daughter. While in the process of dispatching about thirty bad guys, he gives a whole new level of meaning to the concept "rescuing the beauty."[2]

Why start with that? Well, there are parallels for us. Our families, our wives, and our children are under attack. There is one who is trying to take them and enslave them.

1 Peter 5:8 says, "Be of sober spirit, be on the alert. Your adversary, the devil, prowls around like a roaring lion, seeking someone to devour." Note the objective of the adversary here. It is not his desire to trouble us, give us a hard time, or make life hard. No, his objective is to devour us — to destroy. He hates us because of the relationship we have with Christ.

He goes after our families, our wives, and our children spreading strife, death, and destruction wherever he can. Look at what he did with the very first family. He turned Eve and then Adam against God and each other. Then he placed in the heart of Cain the desire to murder his brother Abel.

Recently, we moved our youngest child, Brian, into his garage apartment at college. This is his third year in college, but his first away from home. We met his neighbor, we will call him Bob, as we moved him in to his garage apartment. Bob then introduced us to his girlfriend, we will call her Sue, with the words, "Sue is here as much as I am." It did not take much imagination to understand the context of their relationship. Brian is playing

---

[2] In *Wild at Heart,* John Eldredge says that deep in his heart, every man longs for a battle to fight, an adventure to live, and a beauty to rescue. That is how he bears the image of God; that is what God made him to be.

Ultimate Frisbee on the college team. They have tournaments out of town on weekends, just as I did when on my college rugby team. "The third half," we called it. And just like I was back then, he is being exposed to drugs, alcohol, and attitudes toward sex that are, shall we say, less than biblical. Is he equipped to handle this? It is too late to ask that now.

John, our oldest, and Jeff, our middle son, were both residence assistants (RA's) at a major university. Jeff was in the band; John was in the university choir and sang in some of the opera productions. As RA's they were continually exposed to students drinking and what Father Mulcahy on M*A*S*H referred to as fraternizing. Additionally, John was exposed to homosexuality in the opera company. He told me once it was hard enough to remember which guy was dating which girl, but now he had to keep track of which guy was dating which guy.

Jeff traveled with the band on road trips to huge venues, including a national championship game. Like John, he told me story after story of young men and women making choices that we pray he never makes. Were Jeff and John equipped to handle that level of exposure? Again, that question could not be asked after they had moved into the dorm.

Our daughter Ranae has been exposed to much of the same at universities she has attended. When she was considering the Art Institute of San Francisco, she had to navigate a war protest on her way to the interview. She he was offered drugs several times on the street and was encouraged to enroll and start classes without consulting us. That does not include the difficulty of growing up female in a culture that continually promotes products through sex and promiscuity and pushes and prods girls to become sexually active through every media outlet with which they come in contact. Was she able to resist this assault on her femininity? Too late to ask that question.

Those of us who are blessed to have daughters must deal with a a special level of warfare. Satan really hated Eve and by extension hates all of her daughters. He went after her and not Adam in the garden. She is the source of life. He is the destroyer of life. Think of the level of abuse endured by women in the world. We typically will point to the Islamic nation's treatment of women as barbaric. However, walking by any magazine rack should give you a rapid paradigm adjustment. The cheapening of sex for the purpose of commerce is nothing more than prostitution in a culturally acceptable form. Models sell their bodies to sell everything — I was going to qualify that, but it is truly everything. The enemy of our souls has a special hatred for Eve. He wants to demean her, trivialize her role in life-giving, and cheapen her value as the mother of the race. He cannot give life. He is a murderer from the beginning. So naturally he hates one who can give life.

His hatred extends to our marriages and not just Christian marriages, but all marriages. Marriage is described in Ephesians 5 by Paul as the model of the relationship of Christ and the Church. So the enemy of our Lord and our souls does all that he can to destroy that redemptive model. You will have to agree with me that he has had a great deal of success.

The point of all this is that our kids, our wives, and our marriages are under continual attack. This consists of a pressure from the world which, as Paul says, is trying to squeeze them into its mold. John describes the mold as the lust of the flesh, the lust of the eyes, and the boastful pride of life. We do not have our children long, at the most eighteen years before they leave our primary charge. And after they leave, it is too late to begin to think about how to equip them to withstand the pressure of the world. We must act before that.

We are in a war. The enemy wants to take our families, our wives, our kids; he wants to take us — out.

How does a man respond? In 1 Corinthians 16:13 Paul tells us, "Be on the alert, stand firm in the faith, act like men, be strong." That's encouraging, so memorize the verse. Even meditate on it. Do a word study on the key terms. But how do we do it? And what does that look like on a daily basis? How is one "alert" in this context? As men, we do not actually have a lot of examples to follow. There are not many men who finish well. How many men in their seventies or eighties do you witness who are both walking with God and have built wisely into their families?

Deuteronomy 6:7 says, "These words, which I am commanding you today, shall be on your heart. You shall teach them diligently to your sons and shall talk of them on Sunday at church and sometimes on Wednesday nights." Is that what it says in your Bible? Not in mine either. But that seems to be the model a lot of men are following. The end of the passage actually says that we are to talk of them "when you sit in your house and when you walk by the way and when you lie down and when you rise up." When you work that out, it seems to be just about all the time, which, by the way, makes the assumption that you are talking to your kid, and that you have something meaningful to say. Sitting in the den with the TV on does not really capture the intent of the verse.

Later in the same chapter we are told, "When your son asks you in time to come, saying, 'What do the testimonies and the statutes and the judgments mean which the Lord our God commanded you?' then you shall say to your son, 'Ask your mother.'" Uh, no. It is the expectation of scripture that as fathers we are responsible to explain the Word of God to our children.

The importance of you and me as fathers training our children is ubiquitous in the Bible. We could spend the next couple of hundred pages looking at the references. We won't do that, but we will look at a couple that you may know well.

Let's first look at Proverbs 3:1-12. Throughout the book I will be quoting from the NASB, you may want to compare this to whatever translation you are using for your personal Bible study.

1 My son, do not forget my teaching, But let your heart keep my commandments;

2 For length of days and years of life And peace they will add to you.

3 Do not let kindness and truth leave you; Bind them around your neck, Write them on the tablet of your heart.

4 So you will find favor and good repute In the sight of God and man.

5 Trust in the Lord with all your heart And do not lean on your own understanding.

6 In all your ways acknowledge Him, And He will make your paths straight.

7 Do not be wise in your own eyes; Fear the Lord and turn away from evil.

8 It will be healing to your body And refreshment to your bones.

9 Honor the Lord from your wealth And from the first of all your produce;

10 So your barns will be filled with plenty And your vats will overflow with new wine.

11 My son, do not reject the discipline of the Lord Or loathe His reproof,

12 For whom the Lord loves He reproves, Even as a father corrects the son in whom he delights.

"Wisdom" in the Old Testament is about living life well. The implicit expectation here in Proverbs 3 is that the father is going to train his son in wisdom or living life well. Notice in verse 2 that there are significant benefits to the son in that transfer of wisdom. The author states that it will add both quality and quantity of life to the son. In the past that wisdom transfer was relatively easy. Fathers and sons worked together on farms or in businesses. Since the end of WWII, this transfer has not been as prevalent. The corporate culture has separated fathers from their sons. Instead of working side by side, increasingly since the 1950's, sons have been separated from their fathers. Fathers have been at the office working to support the family. They have been working 60 to 70 hours a week to earn the American dream. When they finally get home, they are spent. Even if the kids are still awake, Dad has nothing left to give.

But it is worse than that. In the fifties and sixties, at least mom was home. Not any longer. Taxes have increased to the point that it is nearly impossible for a couple to purchase a home without both spouses working. That means that children are not only removed from their fathers, but also from their mothers in many cases. Therefore, children and even teens spend the majority of their waking hours with people who do not share their last name, family history, or quite possibly, their values. So not only do sons no longer work alongside their fathers as apprentices, in many instances the relationship that does exist is superficial at best.

Yes, our culture has changed. We live in different times than our parents. We live in different times than those portrayed in the Bible. Has the expectation and the necessity of men building into their sons' lives changed with the culture? Has God's Word changed? Do sons and daughters still need the touch of a father to be most effective in life? In my view, the answers to those questions are a loud no, no, and yes, respectively. Our culture may make the task harder, but it still remains our responsibility.

Probably every message you have ever heard on training children has quoted the next verse:

> Proverbs 22:6
> 6 Train up a child in the way he should go, Even when he is old he will not depart from it.

There is some disagreement on the application of the last part of the proverb. Regardless, the first part is clear. We are to be about the business of training our children.

We could go on. But it is not the purpose of this project to create more unfunded guilt for us dads. There are too many unfunded mandates in the modern church. We are bombarded with meaningless clichés with which we have no idea what to do, other than parrot them at seemingly appropriate times. For example, a bunch of us from the Air Force Base at which I was stationed went to a major discipleship conference in Atlanta. During one of the breaks between messages and workshops, I was sitting in a hall off the lobby reflecting on the conference. One of the airmen who had come with us, I'll call him Glen (not his real name), was walking down the hall toward the area where I was sitting. He didn't see me. He was walking as if in a daze with a look of deep, confused concentration on his face. He told me that he had been talking to someone at the conference about an issue he had struggled with for some time. He paused and frowned as the look of dazed, confused concentration returned to his face.

I said, "He told you that you needed to give it to God, didn't he?"

Glen looked up with a glimmer of hope through the daze and said, "Yeah, he did."

"And you don't have a clue what that means do you?"

Glen slowly shook his head, "No, I don't."

All too often, Christian counsel for struggles falls into this category — advice that sounds great without any clear instructions.

So what do we do as fathers to equip our children to withstand the assaults? Specifically how do we equip them to survive in this world? David gives us some clues in Psalm 78:

> Psalm 78:5-8
>
> 5 For He established a testimony in Jacob And appointed a law in Israel, Which He commanded our fathers That they should teach them to their children,
>
> 6 That the generation to come might know, even the children yet to be born, That they may arise and tell them to their children,
>
> 7 That they should put their confidence in God And not forget the works of God, But keep His commandments,

8 And not be like their fathers, A stubborn and rebellious generation, A generation that did not prepare its heart And whose spirit was not faithful to God.

Here the expectation is that we are passing on to our children the larger story of what God has done, so they will know Him and His majesty. That means the entire sweep of the story and not just the bit in which we dwell. The directive is to let them know what the Lord has been up to in the overall story of redemption, what W. Graham Scroggie calls *The Unfolding Drama of Redemption.*[2] But note the purpose of the instruction; it includes more than just knowledge. In verse 7, Asaph the Psalmist tells us the purpose of our training is that the children would put their confidence in God. Boiled down to its essence, that simply means that they will trust Him. This is huge. We are to share the story of God's involvement in history in a way that causes our children to place their lives completely into His care. That also requires our trust in Him for their lives, but we'll have more on that later.

This instruction and training of our kids reaches beyond just them. It not only results in their personal abandonment to the grace of God, but it also empowers and equips them to repeat the process with their own children and grandchildren. That is a significant assignment with huge multi-generational effects worthy of our focused attention.

But there is more. Look at the next couple of verses.

Psalm 78:9-11
9 The sons of Ephraim were archers equipped with bows,
Yet they turned back in the day of battle.

---

[2] Scroggie, W. Graham. *The Unfolding Drama of Redemption: The Bible as a Whole, Three Volumes Complete and Unabridged in One.* (Grand Rapids, MI: Zondervan Publishing House, 1972).

10 They did not keep the covenant of God And refused to walk in His law;

11 They forgot His deeds And His miracles that He had shown them.

Here were men trained for battle, yet they did not fight. Not only did they not fight, but they also turned away from the battle. I have read that in WWII only 25% of the soldiers ever fired their weapons in battle. It is clearly not enough to pass on knowledge to our children. Since we have an enemy that is committed to our destruction and our kids' destruction, we not only have to train them in content, but we must also train them to engage.

Instruction and training here, then, is clearly not the transference of knowledge or facts in the sense of knowing the content of the Bible, being able to recite the books in order, or being able to find a passage faster than your friend. While all those things are good, they are not the best. The goal of trust here in Psalm 78 helps us avoid the rebuke Jesus gave the Jews in John 5:39-40 which says, "You search the scriptures because you think that in them you have eternal life; it is these that testify about Me; and you are unwilling to come to Me so that you may have life." The whole purpose of our instruction is to know Him, the one behind the Book.

This does not just apply to our physical children, but to those men whom God allows us to mentor.

Paul calls Timothy his true child in the faith in chapter one of I Timothy. We all know and may have memorized:

2 Timothy 2:2: "The things which you have heard from me in the presence of many witnesses, entrust these to faith- ful men who will be able to teach others also."

Notice the same multi-generational impact at work here. The expectation is that we are investing ourselves in both our physical and spiritual sons in a manner that reaches beyond them. The Church has grown through the ages through men investing in their sons and other men.

I am a big fan of the *Andy Griffith Show*. While not overtly Christian, there are a lot of solid biblical values portrayed on the show.

In the episode, *"Bailey's Bad Boy*[3]*"*, Bill Bixby, also known as Bruce Banner in *The Hulk*, and the earthman on *My Favorite Martian*, plays Ronald Bailey, a spoiled rich kid who has broken the law in Mayberry. He runs into a truck belonging to one of the locals and refuses to admit responsibility, pay the fine, or fix the truck. He is waiting for his father's lawyer to spring him.

On Sunday all of the prisoners are taken over to eat at Andy's house. After Sunday lunch, Andy, Barney, Aunt Bea, Opie, and Ronald are on the front porch digesting Aunt Bea's delicious feast. The next course of the meal will be to make homemade ice cream.

Barney and Aunt Bea go into the house to get "the fixin's" for the ice cream. Opie then confides in Andy that he threw a baseball through one of the neighbor's windows. Andy receives the news with his typical restraint and then tells Opie that he will not get his allowance until he pays to fix the damaged window. Meanwhile, Ronald is listening to the conversation.

After Opie goes to help with the ice cream, Ronald asks Andy why he did not cut Opie a break and bail him out since it was just a

---

[3] *The Andy Griffith Show.* "Bailey's Bad Boy," Production Episode #47, Director Bob Sweeney, CBS Television. Original air date: 15 January 1962 (Season 2, Episode 15). Hollywood: Paramount Pictures, 2005, DVD recording.

window. Andy responds, "Oh, yeah, I guess I could just bail him out like you say. But the only trouble with that ...if I was to do that...why every time he got in trouble he'd be expectin' me to come to the rescue. Don't you see? This time it's a broken window, later on it'd be something bigger, then something bigger than that. No, he's got to learn to stand on his own two legs now. No, I've got to keep that young'un straight." Andy walks away and goes to help with the ice cream as Ronald stands there thinking.

In the next scene, Ronald's father's attorney arrives with a scheme to get him out of jail without admitting fault. Ronald refuses, choosing to "stand on his own two legs."

The sequence is a great example of how we are to build both into our sons and into other men. Andy used that moment to teach both Opie and Ronald responsibility. The lessons we build into our sons are the same ones to which all men need to be exposed. As men this is our responsibility to guide and teach not only our sons, but also the men whom God has brought across our paths.

The difficult part here is that we have to have something to pass on and the ability to train. It is not a terribly hard assignment; we do it all the time. For those of us who love to fish, most likely we'll take our kids fishing. Those who love to hunt will go hunting. Those who love college football will go to football games. We tend to involve our family in those things that capture our attention; in activities about which we are passionate.

I love backpacking. So do my kids. Well, my sons do; my daughter, not so much.

I love reading. So do my kids.

I love music. So do my kids. I play guitar, mandolin, and harmonica. All of them play multiple instruments.

I love soccer. My kids have all played. Two competitively.

I love golf, and my kids have all played.

I ride a bike for exercise and have taken the boys on a century tour. Two of them now ride for exercise.

I do not like to fish. I like to hunt, but not all the time the sport takes. My kids did not learn to fish from me. I did take them shooting, but we have not been hunting.

Who we are is what we are going to pass on. We cannot pass on what we do not have. And we won't pass on that for which we have no passion. We reproduce after our own kind.

If we do not have a passion for our Lord, a deep desire to seek Him, we will not pass that on to our children. They may get it, eventually. But it will be from other men.

If we do not have a passion to fight for God's kingdom, we will not pass that on to our children. Again they may get it, but it will not be from us.

We started this chapter looking at Neeson's character in *Taken*. Remember he told the bad guy that he had "a particular set of skills" that he had developed over a lifetime. The skills were his life, and they were intuitive. He had become a dangerous man, able to save his own daughter. What skills do we have? As Christian men, what do we need to be dangerous? What skills do we need to equip our children to not just survive, but engage successfully in this world?

In order to train our kids, we have to start with ourselves. If we want them to walk with God, we have to walk with God. If we want them to study scripture, we have to be men in the Word. Sure, as we have already stipulated, others can give them that training and invest in their lives, but we will be held accountable for our training or lack thereof in the lives of our children. We are stewards, and they are ultimately our responsibility.

There are a number of passages that hint at this:

> I Timothy 3:4-5, 12
> 4 He must be one who manages his own household well, keeping *his children under control with all dignity*
> 5 (but if *a man does not know how to manage his own household*, how will he take care of the church of God?),
> 12 Deacons must be husbands of only one wife, and *good managers of their children* and their own households.

Note the repetition. Each verse emphasizes the importance of managing one's own children, one's household. For a leader in the church, and we are all leaders of our families, there is the expectation that our children are managed well. Part of that includes training them to walk in truth. This is reinforced in our next passage:

> Ephesians 6:4
> 4 Fathers, do not provoke your children to anger, but bring them up in the discipline and instruction of the Lord.

The command here is that we bring up our children in the discipline and instruction of the Lord. It is directed to us as fathers. It is our responsibility. Note how this is contrasted with provoking them to anger. So it follows that the discipline and instruction of the Lord will not provoke anger.

We have already touched on the next verse Deuteronomy 6:7-8. It is so central to our charge as fathers that we need to look at it more closely. Again, it says:

> 6 These words, which I am commanding you today, shall be on your heart.
> 7 You shall teach them diligently to your sons and shall talk of them when you sit in your house and when you walk by the way and when you lie down and when you rise up.

The key here is in the order of the imperatives. Note that the command is for the Word of God to be on our heart first and then taught. It is the Lord's expectation that we are following Him. This is not a case of do what I say, but not what I do. We are to be in the scripture ourselves as we are training our children.

During the workshops we have done over the past two years, one or all of my sons come for the last thirty minutes. The purpose of that time is for the men in attendance to ask them questions about what we have done together. My sons have asked me several times what I want them to say. I have told them each time to answer the questions honestly. And they have. There are things we did with them that did not work. In fact, there are things that they really detested. Sometimes they share about things we did that I frankly do not even remember.

I typically step aside to the background during this portion of the workshop. I found that the questions flow better if I do. I have learned a lot from listening to these exchanges.

One such exchange was a great lesson for me. I do not remember the specific question, but our middle son Jeff answered it. In his answer, he made a statement that rocked me. He was talking to the men about questions that he had about the Bible and what to do in certain circumstances. He told them that he had confidence in me because he knew that I was always doing Bible study. He knew that I was in The Book. Therefore, he felt that he could come to me and get his questions answered effectively, and he knew that I could help him find the right answers.

I did not know he had been watching that closely. But he was. Our kids know what is important to us. They know what we are doing. It impacts them. If we are going to impart a love for the Word into their life, we have to love it ourselves. It is impossible to give someone something that we do not first possess.

And we are going to be held responsible for our walk with God and for our handling of the Word of God.

In 2 Timothy 2:15, Paul tells us, "Be diligent to present yourself approved to God as a workman who does not need to be ashamed, accurately handling the word of truth." This is not a casual undertaking. It takes diligent work. The image here is one of a precise workman. When I was in the seventh grade, we moved from one area of Dallas to a more affluent area. My parents had the house built. One evening, we stopped by to check on the progress of the house, which was common practice. When we arrived, a cabinet maker was in the house looking at the cabinets. As I recall, he was working on another house nearby and was there to observe the work going into our cabinets. I remember him pointing to the joints between the doors and the hinges and talking about the tolerances. He boasted about how he could make the cabinets work with a very small space between the doors and how the space would be consistent from top to bottom. It was pride in expert workmanship. It was precision. It was diligence. When I read this verse, I think of that man's passion. The pride he had in what he did with wood; wood that we know is temporal. Here we are exhorted by the apostle to take that same approach to the eternal Word of God.

In Hebrews 5:12-14, more of our responsibility is brought to light by the author:

> 12 For though by this time you ought to be teachers, you have need again for someone to teach you the elementary principles of the oracles of God, and you have come to need milk and not solid food.
> 13 For everyone who partakes only of milk is not accustomed to the word of righteousness, for he is an infant.
> 14 But solid food is for the mature, who because of practice have their senses trained to discern good and evil.

Observe here that the issue of maturity is not dependent on time. It does not matter how long you have been in the faith. The recipients of this letter had apparently been Christians for some time. However, they were not progressing in their faith. The writer rebukes them saying that they ought to be teachers, but they had not changed their diet. The expectation is that they should have been taking on heavier fare as they matured in the faith. Apparently these people had not chosen to do that. No, they stuck with the milk. Think in terms of our physical bodies. If we do not progress a child from milk to solid food, we will get a visit from child protective services. It would be considered child abuse. It is our responsibility not only to increase the complexity of our diet, but also the diet of our children as they grow in the faith. It is not acceptable for us to allow them to stay stagnant in their diet of the Word of God anymore than it would be to allow them to continue to eat pabulum. If you have children, you may recall that the transition from milk to solid food was resisted. We made spoon airplanes fly into the hangar, tasted it for them to show it was good, cleaned up one food mess after another, and there was much coaxing and patience required to make the change.

The bottom line here in Hebrews is that it's not acceptable for us, our children, or the ones whom we help in the Lord to remain where we are. The expectation is that we are growing. Furthermore, as we have seen previously in Psalm 78 and 2 Timothy 2:2, the expectation is that we are passing what we know on to others.

All of us have known people who reached some pinnacle in their life and parked there. When I was a senior in high school, just shortly after the earth's crust cooled, our basketball team won the state championship. Our point guard sealed the deal with two free throws at the end of the game. He was a hero, and the crowd went wild; you know the story. I went to our 20th reunion and saw him for the first time since we had graduated. He was wearing the same style glasses he wore at the state championship and was still reveling in that past glory. It was rather sad. But how many believers do you know who are living similarly in their spiritual lives. They memorized a verse once and share that same verse every time there is a spiritual discussion. Or they had one experience with God they retell over and over. It is abnormal not to move on and continue to grow.

It is not the objective here to load you up with guilt. The idea is to show you that we are biblically accountable to do the things we are talking about in this book. However, in my experience, the Church today is really good at creating what I call unfunded mandates. As a body we are quick to point out areas that need improvement, but we are not all that quick, or effective it seems, in equipping people to do what we've just told them they are supposed to do. Our purpose here, therefore, is to equip you to do what the Bible says is our responsibility to our children.

So now that we have established that it is our responsibility to fight for and train our kids, where do we start?

We start with ourselves.

CHAPTER 2

Starting With Ourselves

You and I are responsible for our own walk with God. That walk with God is essential if we are going to be successful in the fight for our children. But WE have to do it. No one can walk with God for us.

Personal development does not happen by proxy. We cannot have someone else lift weights and expect that our body will become trim. We cannot watch others run and expect that our cardiovascular system will benefit. We cannot watch others eat and expect to be nourished. We cannot watch others invest or save their money and expect our bank accounts to grow. We cannot watch others work and expect to get their paychecks.

Yet for some reason, it seems there are a lot of us who think if we watch others walk with Christ we will develop a close relationship with Him.

In a couple of Sunday school classes, we examined this principle from the standpoint of courtship. Say as a single man I was interested in a particular gal, in fact, my dream girl. Suppose I asked a friend of mine to spend thirty hours a week with her and then report to me about her once a week for twenty to thirty minutes. During that time, I could not ask any questions, but I could take notes on what my friend chose to tell me about the girl of my dreams. How would my relationship with her proceed? The consensus of the students was that the friend would end up marrying my dream girl. They are right. But the approach I have just described is how it seems a great number of people in the Church approach their relationship with Christ. Far too many of us let the pastor or teacher do the studying and then tell us what they have found. They learn and develop their relationship with Christ through the Word, and we live on their crumbs rather than going to the Word of God ourselves.

There is an old illustration, the hand [see Figure 1], that depicts the different ways we can take in the Word of God. In college ministry we used this illustration all the time. Note that the little finger is "hear," and the little finger is the weakest finger. We cannot get a strong grasp of the Bible if we are only using that finger. Holding something with only your pinky is absurd. Yet for a lot of Christians, that is their primary input. There are percentages that measure what we retain 24 hours after each of these methods of intake. The illustration is richer when you consider these retention rates. Studies have shown that we only remember 5% of what we hear 24 hours after the fact. The same studies tell us that we recall only 35% of what we study 24 hours later. So if your pastor or teacher studies and presents the sermon or lesson, and you remember only 5% of what is presented 24 hours later, that works out to 1.75% of what they studied. Crumbs.

Figure 1 —
The Hand Illustration

I am not suggesting that hearing what men of God share is not helpful. I have been involved in and have benefited from many such ministries, for example:

Dave Jewitt is a friend who founded Your One Degree. It is a ministry that helps men discover and move into the particular purpose for which God has designed them. I have personally benefited from Your One Degree™ workshops and personal time with Dave. Not only have I benefited, but I have also been trained by Dave to coach other men in Your One Degree™, actively helping men through the process, facilitating three workshops in our church, helping Dave put on workshops in other churches, and presenting workshops with him twice.

You may have encountered the work of John Eldredge and the Ransomed Heart Team through the books *Sacred Romance, Journey of Desire, Wild at Heart, Waking the Dead, Way of the Wild Heart,* and *Walking with God.* Maybe you have even attended their Boot Camps. I have read all of John's books and attended both the Boot Camp and the Advanced Boot Camp. Gary Barkalow, co-founder of Ransomed Heart with John, and I conducted a Boot Camp in Trinidad and Tobago together. I have benefited greatly from the work of these men, and I recommend their ministries and materials frequently.

Speaking of Gary, he left the Ransomed Heart Team in 2008 and started The Noble Heart. His ministry helps men find their calling from God. I have had many conversations with Gary about what he is doing and have done some of the exercises he has developed to help men find their calling. He is gifted in helping men discover the unique calling God has placed on their lives through his "Calling Retreats" and "Calling Intensives." I highly recommend his work and his forthcoming book.

Robert Lewis has contributed greatly to the ministry of fathers to their sons. His book *Raising a Modern Day Knight* is a great resource and has birthed several groups of men who are trying to do a better job of raising their children. His work with "Men's Fraternity" has made an impact on many men. The topics covered are not only exceptionally helpful but also insightful. The men's group at our church has finished year three, *The Great Adventure*, and is continuing to use the material to guide men as they navigate the different roles they fill in life.

Before all of the above-mentioned ministries, there was Promise Keepers, the movement that put thousands of men in stadiums throughout the United States. I personally attended three events.

All these organizations have had an amazing impact. As I mentioned, I have personally participated in and received much benefit from each of them and have been active in using the material in my work with men, both in conducting numerous Christian conferences and in speaking to groups of men.

The problem is, as helpful as these events and ministries are, they cannot substitute for spending time with Christ in the Word. We simply cannot walk with God without it. It does not matter how good the events or books are, they cannot take the place of time in His presence, devouring scripture, hungry for a glimpse of the Savior. To take great liberties with Matthew 7:22-23, "Many will say to Me on that day, 'Lord, Lord, did we not go to all the best conferences, did we not read the most current books, did we not attend the most purpose driven churches, did we not listen to the best Christian music?' And then I will declare to them, 'I never knew you, depart from Me, you who practice lawlessness.'"

We acknowledge and practice this need for direct experience in almost every area of our lives. Americans especially are fiercely independent, not wanting anyone to infringe on their freedoms. Yet in the Christian life, we have all kinds of reasons to get into the Word of God by proxy. You have heard them:

- I can't understand the Bible without help.

- The language is too hard to understand; I get lost in all of the thees and thous.

- I do not know where to start.

- I do not have any training on how to understand it.

- I do not have the time.

The root of these perceived barriers to studying the Word may be a fundamental misunderstanding of the Bible and how to understand it. There are four steps to Bible Study:[1]

- Observation

- Interpretation

- Correlation

- Application

---

[1] These four steps are the elements of inductive Bible study. There is another form of Bible study called deductive which is not covered in this book. Generally, deductive study starts with a position and attempts to validate it. In contrast, generally, inductive study starts with the text and looks to discover what positions should be. While deductive study is useful when used correctly, inductive study is the focus of this book.

There are four questions associated with these steps that we must ask of the text in any Bible study. They are:

- What does it say? (Observation)

- What does it mean? (Interpretation)

- What does it say in other parts of the Bible that help me understand this? (Correlation)

- What does it say that I need to do? (Application)

When I ask groups of people which question to start with, most — I would say greater than 95% will say — "What does it mean?" Usually in a Bible study group that is reading and reacting to a passage, it will be the first question that emerges in some form or another. Therein lay the problem. The questions are taken out of order. In some cases, the first one is never asked.

We cannot know what a passage means if we do not know what it says.

Typically, when we take the time to look at what the text says, the meaning is fairly clear.

But for whatever reason it seems like some believers approach the scripture with a level of trepidation thinking there is code embedded in the text or a special thing one has to do to understand what it is saying. No. Not at all. The Bible is a library of books written to people for the purpose of communicating to them. Most of the New Testament books were letters written to individuals or churches to deal with specific issues that had come up in their lives as they tried this walking with Christ thing. It was written in the common language of the day, using common vocabulary and grammar. The expectation of the human authors was that their words would communicate. There are exceptions. Some prophecy and the book of Revelation are written with veiled meanings. But even in those passages, there is much to be understood just by observing what the text says. I tend to agree with Mark Twain who said, "It ain't those parts of the Bible that I can't understand that bother me, it is the parts that I do understand," because it is those that I have to apply to my life.

Mostly, the Bible just means what is says.

It is a tremendously instructive study to look at what the Bible says about itself. If we look up all the passages that have references to the Word of God, His commandments, precepts, laws, etc., we gather quite a substantial list. To reinforce the necessity of getting in the Word for ourselves, we will take the rest of the book to go through each verse in detail. Not really. Let's look at four.

I Peter 2:2

"...like newborn babies, long for the pure milk of the word, so that by it you may grow in respect to salvation,"

Have you ever negotiated a feeding with a newborn? You know how it goes. The baby is crying, but you are in the middle of your favorite show. So you walk over to the expressive child and say, "Honey, I realize that you are hungry. I'll tell you what, we are 15 minutes into the show, so I will get back to you with your formula in...oh say, 45 to 50 minutes." How exactly would that work out for you? Right. Babies do not negotiate, exercise reasonable judgment, or show restraint when it comes to their demand for nutrition. They want what they want, and they want it right now.

Their focus is intense, unwavering, and consuming to the point that they are sometimes exhausted by their demands and fall asleep eating.

Peter says this is to be our attitude toward the Word of God; demanding to get it, not satisfied until we are partaking of its riches. We are to fight, to press into His truth. It is to be our necessary nourishment. In Job 23:12 this attitude is echoed, "I have not departed from the command of His lips; I have treasured the words of His mouth more than my necessary food." Read that again. Job says the Word of God is more important than food necessary to sustain life! When is the last time you skipped breakfast so you could dive into the Word? Our attitude toward the Bible should be that it is critical for our survival.

Why?

Because it is. Note the reason that Peter says we are to have this attitude toward our spiritual food. "So that...," which is a structural marker identifying purpose: "by it." A further structural marker denotes agency, "you may grow...." Did you get that? The purpose of our attitude is to get into the Word of God so that it will enable our growth. If we are to grow as a believer, it is required that we are regularly taking in and digesting the Word of God.

Hebrews 5:12 – 14

"For though by this time you ought to be teachers, you have need again for someone to teach you the elementary principles of the oracles of God, and you have come to need milk and not solid food. For everyone who partakes only of milk is not accustomed to the word of righteousness, for he is an infant. But solid food is for the mature, who because of practice have their senses trained to discern good and evil."

There are several key concepts in this passage that will help us get a handle on our responsibility toward the Word of God. Back to our example in Chapter 1, the first concept is that maturity is not a function of time. In the first part of the passage, the writer of Hebrews chastises his readers. He tells them that for the time they have been in the faith, they ought to be at a point that they are helping others grow through teaching. Pause. Think about that for a minute. Time in grade does not equal advancement. The passing of seasons does not mean growth. Although time is required, it's simply not enough. Think about the newborn we tried to talk out of eating in 1 Peter 2; if the baby just had time alone, it would die. The baby needs time and food to grow. So do we. Food and time.

But not just any food will do. The writer attributes his readers lack of growth to their steady diet of pabulum. In 1 Peter we are to have an appetite like a young baby for its milk. But here we see that we are not supposed to stay there. How would you react to a 24-year-old drinking formula from a bottle or eating strained carrots? In shock, of course. That is what was happening in the community. The author's expectation is that the believers in this region would progress to more and heartier fare as they progressed in their journey as Christ's followers. In fact, it is this progression from milk to meat over time that would have fueled their development. What an interesting dynamic. If believers do not progress, they do not stay where they are, rather they regress to the point that they need to be told the elementary things again.

A good diet is not sufficient by itself either. They not only were to increase the quality of their intake of the Word, but the writer of Hebrews was also instructing these believers to practice what they learned from that exercise. Diet and exercise. We kind of get tired of hearing it, don't we? It sounds like James 1:22–25, "But prove yourselves doers of the Word, and not merely hearers who delude themselves. For if anyone is a hearer of the word and not a doer, he is like a man who looks at his natural face in a mirror; for once he has looked at himself and gone away, he has immediately forgotten what kind of person he was. But one who looks intently at the perfect law, the law of liberty, and abides by it, not having become a forgetful hearer but an effectual doer, this man will be blessed in what he does."

So the picture emerging of what we should be like thus far is of people who crave the Word of God in increasing quantity and quality and who habitually apply what they are learning from their resulting interaction. The natural result of this activity is that we become teachers, not just of our families but of other believers as well.

There is another principle that seems to emerge from these passages. While it is expected that we have this type of craving and interaction with these results from the Word of God, it is also apparently true that we need to be reminded continually. Both Peter and the author of Hebrews had to tell their readers that they were to have these attitudes even though they should have been naturally occurring. So it seems that while the attitudes and actions described in 1 Peter 2 and Hebrews 5 should be normal, it is actually normal for us as believers to require prodding and reminders to engage in this behavior. Prod. Prod. Yes, we need help. We need people who care about us to remind us what we should be doing and what we should be craving.

2 Timothy 3:14–17

"You, however, continue in the things you have learned and become convinced of, knowing from whom you have learned them, and that from childhood you have known the sacred writings which are able to give you the wisdom that leads to salvation through faith which is in Christ Jesus. All Scripture is inspired by God and profitable for teaching, for reproof, for correction, for training in righteousness; so that the man of God may be adequate, equipped for every good work."

The first part of the passage is what Dr. Hendricks[2] refers to as the obstetric function of the Word of God. Interaction with the Bible leads to salvation. This is powerful.

While I was in the Air Force, I memorized several verses that dealt with common excuses or questions people had about becoming Christians. While training to be an instructor pilot, there were a couple of men in my class with whom I had shared the Gospel. One weekend one of the men and I went waterskiing at a lake near my parent's house. We stayed in an upstairs room with twin beds. Saturday night as we were turning in, I pulled out my Bible and was reading it before we went to sleep. My friend started peppering me with questions. Rather than answer them, I would

---

[2] Howard Hendricks is the Distinguished Professor, Chair, Center for Christian Leadership, at Dallas Theological Seminary. Dr. Hendricks is referred to as "Prof" by those who have had him in class. So if you see "Prof" later, it is Hendricks.

turn to the passage I had memorized, which answered the question. Then I would hand him the Bible across the nightstand between the twin beds. He would read the passage and ask another question. I would take the Bible back, turn to the passage I had memorized that answered that question, and then hand him back the Bible saying, "Read this." This went on for more than an hour. At the end he had exhausted his questions. Sometime in that next week he trusted Christ. It was the power of the Word of God that brought him to Christ.

About two weeks later, the other guy and I were walking across the base. Similarly, he was asking a lot of questions. I did not have a Bible with me so I quoted the verses to him as we walked. Then we would discuss the answer the verse suggested and he would pose another question. Again this went on for about an hour. The next week he trusted Christ. Again - it was the power of the Word of God.

But that is not all this verse tells us. The reason this power is there is revealed in the second half of the passage. Paul tells us that, "All scripture is inspired by God...." *Inspired* here in Greek is "theopneustos," which is comprised of two Greek roots: theo = God and pneustos = breathed. Therein lay the reason that it had the effect on those men and has the same effect on us and those with whom we share it. It is the God-breathed power of God in written form.

Then Paul tells us that the Word of God is profitable, and he gives us the particulars of its profit. He tells us that the Word teaches us. It teaches us how to pray, how to react to enemies, how to love, and how to walk with Christ.

It reproves us, though that is not a word that we usually employ. This means that it tells us when we get off the right path. Wow. As we are in the Word of God, the Holy Spirit will shine His light on things that we have done that do not align with His will.

Paul then tells us that the Word of God corrects us. So after the Holy Spirit shows us where we have gone wrong, He gets us back on the right path; He shows us how to change our behavior to realign ourselves with His will.

Lastly, the Word of God trains us. It shows us how to walk on the right path with our God.

The verse can be illustrated by the following diagram:

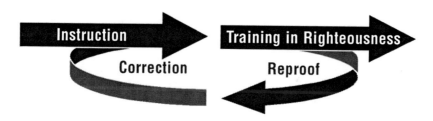

Paul then reveals the purpose of these four functions of the Word of God. It is so we can be adequate and equipped for every good work. So the only means of being effective in the Christian life is being in the Word of God.

John 15:7

"If you abide in Me, and My words abide in you, ask whatever you wish, and it will be done for you."

The context of this passage gives it considerable weight. It is interesting that John devotes seven of his twenty-one chapters to the Last Supper, betrayal, crucifixion, and burial. Of that seven, five are the last discourse with the disciples, and this verse is close to the middle of those five chapters.

Chapter 15 is sandwiched between the two chapters that promise the Holy Spirit. One of the key words in this passage is *abide*, in Greek, *meno*. The word appears eleven times in Chapters 4 through 16, it means to remain or dwell. It gives the sense of staying put. Christ is saying that we are to dwell in His Word. We are to remain in it. This is not a one time thing, but it is a continual state.

Note the result of remaining and dwelling in the Word; we can ask and it will be done, we will bear fruit and the fruit will continue. The word again is *abide.*

It is the Lord's expectation and delight that we remain in His Word.

So, working backward through the passages, we have to remain, dwell, and abide in His Word if we want to be adequate in the Christian life. Of course, that would include leading our children in the Word of God. We have to be continually growing in our intake of the Word with an attitude of craving it like a hungry baby.

That about sum it up?

So now, let's get back to the excuses....

Like me, you may have heard some of these excuses, or others, on why men are not studying the Bible. I am not talking about a reading plan here or a devotional time there. I am talking about in-depth study — work, the same level of work that we put into our careers. I am talking down and dirty work, equipped with nothing more than a pen and a blank sheet of paper, and digging into the

Word of God on your own with the leading and guidance of the Holy Spirit.

Someone may respond, "But that is the domain of pastors, Sunday school teachers, etc. It is not for the common Christian to dive into the Word like that." Since this is a Christian book, I cannot respond to that the way I would have several years ago, but to paraphrase Colonel Sherman T. Potter — that is a load of horse biscuits. Acts 17:11 tells us, "Now these were more noble-minded than those in Thessalonica, for they received the word with great eagerness, examining the Scriptures daily to see whether these things were so." "These" were not the synagogue leaders; they were the men who attended the synagogue. And notice that they did not just read it, they studied it. They took it upon themselves to check out what Paul was telling them in the scripture for themselves. They were checking up on what Paul said by studying the scrolls for themselves. They did not take what he told them about Christ uncritically; they did not assume he was right just because he spoke with authority.

Neither should we uncritically accept what someone says on radio, television, or from a pulpit. No one who is worth their salt and speaks from one of these venues would disagree. However, most of the men or women who speak from these venues seem to have lost the purpose of their gifts. While they are encouraged to teach and preach by the Word, Ephesians 4 tells us that the main purpose of these gifts is to equip the saints. Equipping is not the same as teaching. There is an old, apparently Chinese (according to Google) proverb, "Give a man a fish and you feed him for a day. Teach a man to fish and you feed him for a life-time." That is a great example of equipping.

Romans is considered the pinnacle of Christian doctrine. It was not written to pastors. It was not written to theologians. It was not written to seminary professors. It was not written to philosophers. It was written to a church. It was written to people like you and me, normal folks, with the expectation that normal folks would be able to understand it. Sure, it can be hard to understand as Peter said in 2 Peter 3:15-16, but we need to try.

When was the last time you did something worth doing — and it was easy?

It is not easy. But it is essential to leading our kids in the Word.

In the movie *Kingdom of Heaven*[3], Liam Neeson plays Godfrey, the father of Orlando Bloom's character Bailian. Bailian was the illegitimate son, the result of an affair forced on his mother by Godfrey. Bailian's wife has recently committed suicide after the death of her child, and Bailian does not know Godfrey is his father. Godfrey shows up shortly after Bailian's wife's death, and he asks Bailian's forgiveness for not being in his life. He invites him to leave the obscurity of his blacksmith shop and join him in the larger story as his heir, fighting with him in the crusades.

---

[3] *Kingdom of Heaven.* Director Ridley Scott, Twentieth Century Fox. Beverly Hills, CA: Twentieth Century Fox Home Entertainment, 2006, DVD recording, 4 Disc Director's Cut. The scenes referenced are (time stamps) Disc 1: 14:50 – 19:40, Godfrey calling Bailian out of obscurity; 22:34 – 27:22, Godfrey teaching him to defend and defending him; 38:16 – 40:56; Godfrey commissioning Bailian. Disc 2: 47:03 – 49:24, Bailian commissioning the men in Jerusalem. While there is some question about the historical veracity of the film, this story arc is worth the price of the DVD. There are more good character issues that are shown through the development of the character of Bailian plus opportunities to talk about purity. Do not use the film with your child without viewing it first. The time invested will be worth it.

Bailian initially declines. However, after killing his priest brother for having his wife's corpse beheaded, he joins his father's band.

The first thing Godfrey does after Bailian joins him is evaluate his ability with a sword. He adjusts the way that he holds his sword and the guard he uses. He instructs him to never take a low guard, but always a high guard. He demonstrates and explains why it is a superior way for him to wield his sword. Then he has him practice this first against himself and then against one of his men. While this is happening, authorities are coming to arrest Bailian for the murder of the priest. One of Godfrey's men is on the outskirts of the camp, and he is killed by a crossbow bolt while Godfrey is working with Bailian. When the men come into the camp to arrest Bailian, Godfrey refuses to allow them to arrest him. A fight ensues, and while defending his son, Godfrey receives a wound that later proves fatal.

Just before Godfrey dies, he passes on his barony to Bailian and administers the oath of a knight, giving him his ring and sword. The oath is a key part of the movie: "Be without fear in the face of your enemies. Be brave and upright that God may love thee. Speak the truth always, even if it leads to your death. Safeguard the helpless and do no wrong. That is your oath."

Bailian takes his father's position in Jerusalem. At the end of the movie he is called upon to defend the city and protect the people. While preparing for the coming battle, the patriarch complains to Bailian that they cannot defend the city because there are no knights. The following scene occurs:

> **Balian of Ibelin:** Truly? [He looks around him at the men standing by; his gaze falls on a young man] What is your condition?

Young Man: I am servant to the Patriarch.

Bishop, Patriarch of Jerusalem: He's, uh, one of my servants.

Balian of Ibelin: Is he? You were born a servant? [The young man nods his head yes] Kneel. [Bailian watches as the young man kneels, then turns and speaks to the men.] Every man at arms or capable of bearing them, kneel. [All men kneel, Bailian turns and walks to the young man. He yells out.] On your knees! [All that can be seen are kneeling, and Bailian looks down at the young man]

At this point Bailian administers the oath quoted above to all the kneeling men. He continues:

Balian of Ibelin: Rise a knight! Rise a knight! [He turns and sees the gravedigger who beheaded and buried his wife], Master gravedigger.

Gravedigger: It is you.

Balian of Ibelin: Not what I was, nor are you. Rise a knight.

Bishop, Patriarch of Jerusalem: [almost crying] Who do you think you are? Will you alter the world? Does making a man a knight make him a better fighter?

[The camera pans at this point to show the faces of the men in the area. There is a noticeable pride on their faces. As Bailian is walking away, he halts, turns slowly.]

Balian of Ibelin: Yes.

This story arc closely parallels the charge and the hope we have as fathers. While it focuses on the transmission of mission to sons, there are similar and in some ways more important issues we need to transmit to our daughters. Godfrey calls Bailian into manhood, equips him to fight, and commissions him in the battle. Bailian then takes his commission and raises other men to fight in the battle. Epic. Stunning. It is my dream for my sons and my daughter: to equip them not only to fight well in the battle, but also to raise other men and women to fight with them. It is a great picture of 2 Timothy 2:2, "The things which you have heard from me in the presence of many witnesses, entrust these to faithful men who will be able to teach others also."

We are in the midst of a battle. And like Godfrey's camp, men on the edges are getting picked off by the enemy who roars around like a roaring lion seeking someone to devour. There are even some getting picked off in the middle of the camp. Why? They are not taking a high guard. They are not daily taking up the Sword of the Spirit.

In order to fulfill our purpose and assist our sons and daughters in their purpose, we are required to correctly handle the weapons we fight with for His kingdom. Godfrey was an expert with his sword, and he was battle-tested. He had not learned to use it by watching programs about the crusades on the military channel. He was in the crusades and was expert with his sword. He knew how to use it for maximum benefit. He was, therefore, able to equip his son.

As fathers we have the same responsibility as Godfrey. You may say that you have not been in battle. Yes, you have. You have lived life longer than your son or daughter. It may be that you have not lived your life under the influence of the sword of the Spirit, the Word of God. That is easily remedied. God is sovereign, and He is gracious. If this describes you, there is a fresh start available now. It is the purpose of this book to help you begin and sustain that quest.

Some of the ministries to which I referred earlier advocate giving our sons replicas of swords as a reminder that they are to be warriors and fight well. What a great idea. I have one hanging in my office. If you come to one of my workshops, you will see it. I use it along with showing the scenes from *Kingdom of Heaven* to illustrate the importance of a firm grasp on the Word of God.

But the symbolic sword will not help us nor our sons fight well against the enemy, nor will they help us defend our families. But they are a valuable reminder, a prodding.

In Matthew 4:1-11, Christ models confrontation with the enemy:

1 Then Jesus was led up by the Spirit into the wilderness to be tempted by the devil.

2 And after He had fasted forty days and forty nights, He then became hungry.

3 And the tempter came and said to Him, "If You are the Son of God, command that these stones become bread."

4 But He answered and said, "It is written, 'Man shall not live on bread alone, but on every word that proceeds out of the mouth of God.' "

5 Then the devil took Him into the holy city and had Him stand on the pinnacle of the temple,

6 and said to Him, "If You are the Son of God, throw Yourself down; for it is written, 'He will command His angels concerning You'; and 'On their hands they will bear You up, So that You will not strike Your foot against a stone.' "

7 Jesus said to him, "On the other hand, it is written, 'You shall not put the Lord your God to the test.' "

8 Again, the devil took Him to a very high mountain and showed Him all the kingdoms of the world and their glory;

9 and he said to Him, "All these things I will give You, if You fall down and worship me."

10 Then Jesus said to him, "Go, Satan! For it is written, 'You shall worship the Lord your God, and serve Him only.'"

11 Then the devil left Him; and behold, angels came and began to minister to Him.

We are all very familiar with this passage. You have probably already noticed that each time Satan attacked Christ, Christ parried the thrust with the sword of the Spirit, the Word of God. But look at the second time Satan attacked, in verse 6. Satan actually quotes the Bible. He attempts to use scripture against Christ Himself. The implications of this are huge. Our enemy knows the Word of God and will not hesitate to use it. He quotes it still today. There are multiple ways the enemy has twisted scripture and deceived people. Some of the cults — The Way, Jehovah's Witnesses, and the Mormons are evidence of this. In the Church, we find followers who add requirements for salvation beyond simple faith in Christ. We have to really know scripture to be able to fight successfully against his tactics.

You may say, "It is hopeless, I could never learn to handle the Word of God like that." Yes, you can. If you are a believer, you have the Holy Spirit and Christ's promise that the Holy Spirit will guide you into all truth. The Lord honors those who come to Him in faith. Not only does He honor them, He also protects them and monitors the attacks the enemy throws at them so they are not overwhelmed. First Corinthians 10:13 says, " No temptation has overtaken you but such as is common to man; and God is faithful, who will not allow you to be tempted beyond what you are able, but with the temptation will provide the way of escape also, so that you will be able to endure it."

This looks a lot like what we are told to do in James 4:10, does it not? "Submit therefore to God. Resist the devil and he will flee from you." If we have Jesus' model of battle in Matthew 4 and

James' exhortation on how to battle in James 4, is it not reasonable to conclude that part of submission to God and resistance of the enemy is skill with God's Word? We must be able to take a high guard with the sword of the Spirit

The issue is we typically have not been equipped to do this. Sure, some of us have been in Bible studies. We have read books that people have written about the Bible, like *40 Days of Purpose.* We may have been in groups that read a passage in the Bible and reacted to it. We may have been in Bible studies that use workbooks, where we fill in the blanks. Or we have tried to study something on our own and find ourselves spending more time reading the notes in our study Bibles and commentaries than the actual Bible.

But in-depth study is not the same. The purpose here is to show you that you can start with the Bible and a blank sheet of paper and take a high guard with the sword of the Spirit.

So are you convinced you need to do this? Ready to get going? So what do you do?

CHAPTER 3
What to Do

Start

So what do we do? Start. Get up. Get moving. Begin.

The second semester of my first senior year at Texas A&M (there were two senior years, since I crammed four years of education into five), several of my friends began playing rugby. I went to one of their practices to check it out. Practices for the A&M rugby team consisted of about a two-hour game pitting the first team against the second team. As I talked to the coach about my interest in the game, he told me to get on the field. I protested that I did not know anything about rugby; he told me the best way to learn was to start at fullback. He assured me that if I messed up, the other players would let me know. They did.

A year and a half later, I graduated having played hundreds of hours of rugby, including practices, games, and tournaments. My position changed around, but the method of learning did not. My teammates continued to be my best instructors and coaches. I even learned a lot from my opponents.

The point here is that the coach did not give me a whole lot of instruction before he chucked me into the game. In fact, I had none. He wanted me to just get started and not think too much about it just engage.

Getting started is the hardest part of doing anything new that is not a habit. No amount of planning or thinking about it will substitute for actually starting. Newton called it inertia. You know the definition, "a body at rest tends to stay at rest..." While he was talking about physics, this concept applies to our spiritual lives as well. It is tough getting started. We come up with all kinds of delaying tactics to keep from actually doing something. Most of the reasons will take the form, "After I _____, I will get started." You can insert almost anything you would like into the blank. The problem is, as soon as _____ is done, another _____ gets in the way. So just start.

Start Small

In the next chapter we are going to look specifically at where to start, but right now the concept is to start small. The Bible is a big book. The version I use is 1749 pages. There are 66 books, which represent several different kinds of literature. It is a bit like walking into a library for the first time with the intent to get a handle on the entire collection. It can be somewhat daunting.

Think about what you do for a living. If you are an engineer, you did not start by designing a project. You started in math and graphics. Bit by bit you added different courses, until in your senior year you approximated a project. If you have become registered, you have practiced for several years under the tutelage of senior engineers, and then sat for an exam to obtain your registration. It took time; it took discipline; it took study; it took getting help. This same pattern will fit just about any profession. You start small. And when you start small, you make mistakes. You know, the best golfer in the world was once a beginner.

As adults with some success in a field, it can be humbling to start something new in which we do not have a lot of experience or knowledge. It is hard to admit that we need help; heck, it is hard to ask for directions. The fact is, we are not all experts in everything. If this is your first shot at studying the Bible by yourself, you may feel uncertain you are getting the right results from your study. And that's OK. At some level the process and the effort is just as important as getting the "right" answer.

So be patient. Give yourself some slack — grace if you want to use a biblical term. The Lord is excited to meet with you where you are.

Start Daily

If you have ever gone through the process of learning a foreign language, you know that doing a little work daily has a large impact on the speed and effectiveness of your learning. The same is true in studying the Bible. Start by setting some time aside each day to dig in to God's Word. Based on your schedule, pick a time when you are most alert, you can control the interruptions, and you can protect. By protect, I mean that you can be relatively sure people will not schedule something over that time, or that you will have the freedom to say no to those who try (more on that later).

There are two things you should consider doing with this time: devotional and study.

Devotional

You may have heard that you should be having a daily devotional, but you may not have been told what to do. Simply put, this is a time for you to check in with the Lord and just enjoy His presence. There is not a right or wrong way to have a devotional life. It is personal worship and time with the Lord. It is for you and Him, not others. Typically it will include time in prayer and reading scripture. The simplest thing to do is follow a PRP pattern where P is prayer and R is read. So the pattern is Pray, Read, Pray. The first P is to pray and ask the Lord to lead you as you read. Then read, R, for a few minutes in your Bible. There are reading plans available and can be found on my website. Or, you can read the chapter of Proverbs for that day of the month. There are 31 chapters in Proverbs. So, if it is the 6th you read Chapter 6.[1] You do not need to read the entire chapter. If you find a verse that really intrigues you, stop and think and pray through that verse.

Close your time with the second P. You can simply thank God for the time together or ask Him to show you how to use the verse you read during your day. An acronym that has helped some people learn how to pray effectively is ACTS: A is adoration; you praise God for who He is and what He has shown you in the Word. C is confession; you confess any known sin in your life and ask Him for forgiveness. T is thanksgiving; you thank Him for His gifts and provision for you. S is supplication; you ask for your needs and the needs of others for whom you wish to pray.

This method is simple. You will find that these times will build on themselves. Things that you saw or read one day will come to mind to illuminate what you are reading at the time. The more you continue, the richer the experience will be. There will be times when you feel like you are going through the motions. If we are honest, that is true in every relationship we have. It is a part

---

[1] Later on in this book, I explain how to read through all of Psalms in one month's time.

of life. The difference here is that we are dealing with One who can help us understand what is going on. Through prayer, tell Him you are struggling and ask Him what to do about it. Be quiet and listen then to what comes to mind.

You should be able to do this in between seven and ten minutes. The Navigators had a publication called, "Seven Minutes with God" that was very similar to this. We are not talking about a great deal of time here. It is a small investment that will reap great dividends.

Study

The second thing you should consider doing with this time is study. Again, we are not talking about a really protracted time here, but just a consistent effort. There is a really simple way to get started, as easy as ABC. As a matter of fact it is ABC.

A is analyze. Take a portion of scripture and analyze it. On a piece of paper or your journal (we will say more about a journal in a bit), jot down a few notes about what you see in the passage you are reading. You can do this with a paragraph, chapter, or verse. What stands out to you about what you are reading? What questions does the passage raise? Is there anything suggested that you need to do? Are there any behaviors that you need to change? Are there words you do not understand? Feel free to interact with the text. Write down your thoughts.

B is best verse. From the passage you have analyzed, which verse is the one that seems to be the most important? This is not a technical question. That is, you are not looking for what your high school or college English professor would label as the "topic sentence." Rather, it is the thought that is speaking to you where you live right now. Make a note of that verse.

C is contract. What are you going to do with what you have read? How can you live out this interaction with the Word of God? Write down something that you can do with what you have studied. It may be something really simple like memorizing your best verse. It could be something that is more involved like asking for the forgiveness of someone you have wronged. Pray about what the Lord would have you to do with what you have read.

Make sure you pace yourself during this time. Do not try to tackle a bigger chunk of scripture than you will be able to cover in the time you have allotted.

Make Room

You and I, as well as everyone else on the planet, are equal in one thing. We each have 168 hours at our disposal each week. The thing that differentiates us is how we choose to use those hours. In order for you to do something new, you are going to have to do something different. Seems obvious. Don't let that keep you from starting. You may have to get up earlier or go to bed later. You may have to choose not to watch a favorite television show.

OK, in the interest of full disclosure, there is one show on television that I will not miss. However, I refuse to watch it when it is broadcast. Why? If I watch the show when it comes on I have to sit through the commercials. For an hour show that is twenty minutes. So I record the show when it comes on, and watch it later and fast forward through the commercials. It saves me twenty minutes. That is twenty minutes that I can use to study or read.

The point is that you will need to schedule your study. You may have to rearrange or cancel some other activities in order to add this to your routine.

Make it a Priority

Making room on your schedule for regular Bible study assumes that you have made it a priority. If it is not, then you will not continue. When something "better" comes up, you will drop the study from your schedule.

There will be times in life when you will have to skip. Things do happen. In actuality, a lot of the things that we consider urgent are really not that important. They may present themselves as urgent, but there is really very little that comes our way that demands immediate attention. Most can wait until we have time in the schedule.

That for which you are willing to change your schedule is that which you deem most important.

Make a Place

Another thing that will help you in getting started with regular Bible study is to have a place that you will regularly go to for your study. It can be your office, a favorite restaurant, or a coffee shop. It just needs to be a place where you can concentrate without distraction.

I study primarily in my office. I have all of my reference books in there as well as my computer and memorabilia from ministries and mission trips. I can close and lock the doors to keep the family out, and I have a set of noise canceling headphones to block the noise of life.

There is also a coffee house and a restaurant at which I like to study. I use the headphones there as well. The advantage for me is the change of scenery.

Bottom line? You need to have a place where you feel comfortable, where you can concentrate, and where you know that you are going to study. It will enhance your focus and thus your time with the Lord.

Start with Other Men

I have done several workshops with the purpose of helping men lead their children in the Word. In the fall of 2009, there was a workshop at a large church in northwest Oklahoma City. The interaction at this workshop was different than others we have had. As I interacted with the men during the workshop and reflected on this difference over the following weeks, the reason became apparent. These men were walking together through life. They were not in what has been termed an "accountability group"; they were living life together. And it seemed to have at least two great effects for these men.

Encouragement

In Hebrews 3:13, we are told, "But encourage one another day after day, as long as it is still called "Today," so that none of you will be hardened by the deceitfulness of sin." What I saw with these men is that they were able to shore one another up because they were walking through life together. When they had questions about what to do with their sons or daughters, they were able to lean on each other as they figured out together what needed to be done. I have a friend in another state who, like me, has older children. Lately, he has been facing issues with one of them. We have spent time on the phone discussing options, and I have been able to encourage him in things that he is too close to the situation to see.

It is the case sometimes, when it comes to our kids, that our intense desire for them to do well can cloud our ability to see what they need from us. It is then that we need a band of brothers around us who can encourage us with their perspective.

Not Accountability

This is not about someone checking up on you or holding you accountable to some schedule or standard of care. It is about having a group of men who are openly struggling with the same issues. How, in the name of all that is good and right, do we raise children who are walking with God in purity, in the midst of a post Christian, sexually addicted culture? It will take more than you and your wife's abilities to do that.

Through the years, my kids have passed around cars. It started with a Berretta we received from one of the cousins, a '94 Ford Explorer, and the ultimate — an '86 Fiero. My sons all drove the Fiero. My daughter and my wife would not go near the car. The point is, the car was so distinctive that most of the people in our area knew who drove the car. I have gotten calls from friends when the car was seen broken down (frequent calls) before my sons could even call me. The Fiero is a two-seater. One evening a phone call came in from one of our friends at church. With a chuckle in his voice, he asked me if I knew that our youngest son had just left the church parking lot with four people in the car. With all of our children we have a signed driving contract that outlines what is permissible during their use of the car and what is not. Driving the Fiero with four people inside fit into the "what is not" category. Later that evening, my son was practicing piano. I came up beside the piano and said, "Is it your suspicion that people do not know who owns the Fiero?" I told him that he had been caught and we talked about the repercussions.

Yes, I too need other people in my kids' lives. People who I know have the same values and know what I am trying to accomplish. That is one of the benefits of doing this alongside other men.

Gifts Involved

One other benefit of doing this in a community of men is that you will have the benefit of their gifts as you work through issues together. Paul tells us in Romans 12 that we have been given gifts that differ. We are intended to work together to build each other up, according to Ephesians 4. When we face issues in our families we are, at some level, constrained by our experiences and gifts. Having other men around that know us and our families gives us the benefit of their perspective through their experiences and gifts. That can give us valuable insight into different ways to approach the situation and help us see things that we are missing.

Start with Prayer

Diving into the Word is more than an academic exercise or a mental challenge, it is a spiritual endeavor. While we have to engage our reasoning in order to understand scripture, reason alone will not enable us to understand it. We need help. Fortunately, help has been provided. In John 16:13–15, the Lord assures us, "But when He, the Spirit of truth, comes, He will guide you into all the truth; for He will not speak on His own initiative, but whatever He hears, He will speak; and He will disclose to you what is to come. He will glorify Me, for He will take of Mine and will disclose it to you. All things that the Father has are Mine; therefore I said that He takes of Mine and will disclose it to you." One of the jobs of the Holy Spirit is to reveal the heart of Christ to us. He will open the Word of God through illuminating our hearts to the truth it contains. So one of the essential elements in digging into the Word of God for yourself is to pray. Pray and ask the Lord to lead you through your study, to guide you into all truth, and to keep you from error. The exciting thing is that this prayer is consistent with the role of the Holy Spirit and the desire of Christ. 1 John 5:14–15 tells us, "This is the confidence which we have before Him, that, if we ask anything according to His will, He hears us. And if we know that He hears us in whatever we ask, we know that we have the requests which we have asked from Him." Since we know that this is the Holy Spirit's role and the desire of the Lord, we can be sure that this is a prayer that will be answered in the affirmative.

Start a Journal

One of the other things that may help you on this journey is to begin to write down in a journal what you are experiencing. I know. This sounds like work. But there are at least two really good reasons to dive in with a journal.

Judges 2:7, 10 – 11, tells us, "The people served the Lord all the days of Joshua, and all the days of the elders who survived Joshua, who had seen all the great work of the Lord which He had done for Israel. All that generation also were gathered to their fathers; and there arose another generation after them who did not know the Lord, nor yet the work which He had done for Israel. Then the sons of Israel did evil in the sight of the Lord and served the Baals." Note what happened here. When the people remembered what the Lord had done in their lives, they followed Him. When they forgot, they fell into idolatry. Have you ever experienced short term spiritual memory loss? I have. I can have a great day with the Lord, meeting with men, spending quality time in the Word, seeing real answers to prayer. But then I drive out of the Starbuck's parking lot, someone almost kills me with their car. It's amazing how I forget all that has happened previously. I have seen God provide finances miraculously on any number of occasions, yet I still get nervous when the month is looking like it is going to go further than the bank account.

I am learning that a journal helps me remember the faithfulness of God. It does not need to be extensive. Nor does it need to be done every day. But you should be regularly recording what you are learning as you study His Word and discover His faithfulness.

There are those who have really involved systems for journaling, and if that works for you, that is great. It does not work for me. In my journal, all I do is write down the date and time and where I am, and then draw a line across the page under that information. I then record what is happening between me and the Lord in just a few sentences or a few pages. I am a type A personality, driver driver, high D; whatever personality instrument that you are using, I am the risk-taking hardcharger prototype. Being still is not one of my strengths. In my life, I have started several journals. I have them in my library. Five years ago I attended a "Wild at Heart Boot Camp"[1] in Colorado. Part of the event was to spend some extended time with God. They provided us with a small journal to use. I learned during that four-day period that when I sat still and slowed down enough to write what I was thinking, God showed up. It helps me to follow Psalm 46:10: "Be still and know that I am God...."

So the two advantages for me are, first, it helps me keep a record of God's faithfulness to me. Secondly, it helps me slow down and listen to God.

I use a Molskine Plain Notebook, large. I like it for several reasons. First, it has no lines which means I can draw or write sideways. Molskine makes notebooks with lines, I am just not a lines guy. Second, it has a band to keep it closed. Third, it has a ribbon marker. Fourth, it has a cool pocket in the back to put small pieces of paper. Lastly, it is acid-free paper so it will last and the binding is high quality and guaranteed. The first one I had did split. There is a leaflet in the back pocket that tells you if you have a problem to send them a picture by email. I shot a picture with my Blackberry, and they sent me a new journal. Amazing.

One last thing on this: if you are like me when you sit down to be quiet, your internal radio starts blasting. A million ideas flash

---

[1] The "Wild at Heart Boot Camp" is an event put on by Ransomed Heart. The event is four days that focuses on the practical application of John Eldredge's book *Wild at Heart*.

across your mind, or you suddenly remember that you have to check to see if the air in the left rear tire is low. To whose benefit is it if you do not get a good time with the Lord? I am learning that the enemy will flood my mind with great ideas to try to distract me from my time with God. Originally, I tried to keep a list and just refocus on the time with the Lord. I have learned that for me, the list does not work. I am learning to let all of that go and ask the Lord to bring back to mind later what is important. It is yet another area in which I am having to learn to trust the Lord.

Start with a Good Bible

One of the questions that is asked frequently is, "What Bible should I use?" Great question. If you walk into a Christian bookstore you can be overwhelmed by all of the choices; NIV, ESV, NASB, KJV, Message, Living, NKJV, RSV, ad infinitum. So which one is best?

There are a couple of things you may want to consider as you answer this question. First, you need to understand the difference between a version, a translation, and a paraphrase.

Version

A version of the Bible like the King James (KJV) or the New International (NIV) is translated from the original documents by a committee of translators. These scholars meet and debate the best way to render the Hebrew and Greek into the language in which they are translating.

The second thing you need to know about versions is that there are different Hebrew and Greek texts that can be used as the basis of their work. The KJV uses the Byzantine text which is one of the only complete Greek New Testament manuscripts. Most of the other versions will use the NA27 which is an eclectic text compiled by comparing all of the archeological finds to assemble what most scholars believe to be a more accurate Greek text. The introduction to the Bible will tell you what texts were considered in Greek and Hebrew by the committee and what approach they took toward the archeological finds.

Thirdly, the committees have a philosophy of translating that guides the decisions they make. For instance, the King James, Revised Standard, New American Standard, and English Standard Version are literal in their philosophy. That is they attempt to translate as closely as possible word by word from the original texts. In contrast, the New International Version is a dynamic equivalent. The aim of the dynamic equivalent is to attempt to capture the thought of the author rather than what the text says word for word.

Translation

A translation is one person's work in translating the texts into the language in which they are working. Phillips and Wuest are examples of this type of work. Translations all have philosophies driving the translator's work and that should be discernable in the introduction.

Paraphrase

A paraphrase such as the Living Bible, The Message, or Today's English Version, is an author or committee's attempt to capture the thought of the passage and render it into "modern" vernacular. In some cases the paraphrase starts with an English version. In others, they start with the original language. One can read the introductory material to determine the starting point of the particular paraphrase.

Recommendations

Paraphrases and dynamic equivalents are easier to read. However, the nature of the works is that a lot of the ideas and prejudices of the individual that has done the work can color the translation. The same is true of a translation. Since there is no committee by which to vet the work, the individual's bias can peek through their translation. Bias is not completely avoided in a version, but the committee approach can minimize the occurrences.

For study, I would recommend a literal translation. If you choose to use a dynamic version or a paraphrase, I would suggest that you have a literal translation open next to it. Check the versions against one another. If there are significant differences in the way the passages are treated, that is a signal that there are some interesting things happening in the original or that those who created the Bible you are using allowed their bias to creep into the text. Most of the time this will not be an issue, but if you do not have access to the Greek and Hebrew, which most of us do not, comparing versions is a really good way to ensure you are not led astray by the English text.

In my study, I use the NASB in parallel with the Greek NA27[2] for the New Testament and the Hebrew BHS[3] for the Old Testament.

---

[2] NA27 is the *Nestle-Aland Greek New Testament, 27th Edition.*

[3] BHS is the *Biblia Hebraica Stuttgartensia,* it is the standard Hebrew text.

One final recommendation: I would suggest that you not use a study Bible. I will explain why in Chapter Five.

Start Asking Questions

It is an axiom, especially in estrogen rich environments, that men do not ask for directions. There is some truth to that. We tend to be independent by nature. It is one of the ways that God has designed men differently than women. If we look at the roles men fill in the Bible, we can begin to understand some of the reasons for the independence. We were created for domination of our domain, so at some level we assume we should know it. Problem is, we slipped and fell somewhere along the way.

There is a lot that we do not know, especially when we are starting something that we have not done before. As you start this process of studying the Word for yourself, or even if you have been doing this for some time, you will encounter things which you are not sure you understand. Or you may have questions for which you do not have or cannot find answers. First, write the questions down. The act of slowing down enough to think through how to phrase the question will sometimes be enough to get you on track to answering it. Second, make sure that you have taken enough time to observe what the passage says. As we said in Chapter 2, the Bible means what it says most of the time. So make sure you have spent enough time with the text to determine what it says.

Lastly, develop a relationship with someone whom you trust that may have the answer or know how to get it.

We all are on a journey of learning about an infinite God, we need help and we need each other. Ask questions.

Start Leading

This may seem counter intuitive, especially if you are just getting started in Bible Study, but this can really help you grow in your understanding and application of the Word. Lead a Bible study.

Now.

Why? Because as the leader of a Bible study you will be challenged to dig deeper into the Word. As the leader, you have to come up with questions to lead the group. That means that you have to digest the material more than you would if you were just preparing the study for yourself. If you have talked to anyone who has ever led a study, they will tell you that they learned more in that study than the others in the study. Leading forces you to deal with things you may not have considered. Questions will arise for which you have no answers, and it will force you to go back to the Word or those who are helping you in the Word to find answers.

I met Christ in the summer of 1973 just after I entered undergraduate pilot training. I came to Christ through a Bible Study in the bachelor officer's quarters. Six months later I was leading seven Bible studies a week and teaching Sunday school at the base chapel. I do not recommend this, as a matter of fact, I would discourage it. But the Lord used that in my life. Being in front of that many questions about the Word of God each week forced me to study the Bible more effectively, and my understanding of the Word increased rapidly. You may feel that you do not know enough to lead a study. You are right. If you felt that you did, then you would not be qualified. You may be afraid someone will ask you a question for which you do not have the answer. They will. I have a Master's in Theology and have translated most of the New Testament from Greek to English, and I get questions regularly to which my answer is, "I do not know. But give me some time, and I will try to find out."

The subject matter of the Bible is infinite. There is no way that you will ever know enough to feel completely at ease in leading a study. Lead anyway.

Start Teaching

The final suggestion is much like the last one. Teach a Sunday school class or a Bible class. The difference between leading a Bible study and teaching is that in most cases when you teach you are the only one in the room who has prepared. That presents a different set of challenges. It means that you have to lead people though the logic of the text to get to the truths that you are communicating. Also, the types of questions you hear in that setting are of a qualitative and quantitative difference. They will stretch you.

Again, "I don't know," is a legitimate answer.

Start. Get moving. Dive in. Get your feet wet. Risk not getting everything right. The Lord will meet you there. If we are going to invest in the lives of our kids, we have to lead them not only in study, but also by example. Beginning to engage with the Word of God in the ways outlined here will equip you to have a meaningful dialogue with your children on issues with which they are struggling. It will also give you the familiarity with scripture to find the answers to the questions they ask.

Now that you have the framework of what to do, let's pick a place to start.

CHAPTER 4
Where to Start

So you are ready to start. But where? Genesis is not it. The first study I ever did, or the first one I remember doing, was *Studies in Christian Living — Book 4*. It was a Bible study in a barracks at Craig Air Force Base. I still have the book. It is mostly empty. I was not really into the study. At the end of the book, Harry, the first lieutenant leading the study, asked if we were ready to go to the next book. I asked if there was something else we could do. He handed out three sheets of 8.5" x 5.5" paper and suggested we do the study outlined on those three pages. It was a verse analysis study. I went back to my room in the BOQ,[1] and later that week picked up the sheets to start working through the steps. About three hours later I was finished with the study. I had not spent more than about thirty minutes total in the other study. I was literally blown away by the depth of the passage. A few weeks later I trusted Christ.

So you may understand why I am so passionate about getting people into the Word of God.

This Chapter will give you four different ways to approach the scripture. We will look at how and why to study a book as a whole, how to study one verse (where I started), how to study

---

[1] BOQ is Bachelor Officer's Quarters.

one word, and then how to wring one chapter out in a study. Psalms and Proverbs are very different from the other books; after the book as a whole section I will suggest a study approach to Proverbs and a study for Psalms. If you try all of these, there will be little that you cannot do for yourself in the Word of God.

Before we get going on this, I have at least one word of caution or encouragement: do not be intimidated by what you are about to read. If you have never done anything like this, it may seem overwhelming. It is not intended to be. The fact is, anything new we try is awkward the first time. For example, do you remember when you were learning to drive? I remember the first time I drove down a two-lane road in traffic. The speed limit was 70. That meant there was a 140 m.p.h. closure rate with oncoming traffic. I remember that my gut was in a knot. I was nervous and scared that one of those cars was going to come over into my lane, or I would drift into theirs. Today, I will drive down roads like that, drinking a cup of coffee, talking on my cell, not even noticing the oncoming traffic. Why? I have done it thousands of times. Reactions are now second nature; corrections to the direction of the vehicle are second nature. I notice if there is something wrong with the cars coming toward me because I have learned what to expect.

But change just one element — and look out. Several years ago, I was on a mission trip to Indonesia. They drive on the opposite side of the road in Indonesia. There are also a whole lot more bicycles and motor scooters than there are in Texas where I learned to drive. There were two of us on this trip, and one evening we went out to dinner. We borrowed a motor scooter, and I was forced to drive. I did not typically drive a motor scooter in those days, and still do not. On the rare occasions when I had, it was a heavier motorcycle, and I didn't have a 200 + pound man on the back of it. So, to set the stage, I was driving on the left, on a different type of vehicle, with an added burden of a moving passenger. There were road signs in a language I did not understand, and instead of stop signs or lights, there were traffic circles with the rule that if you looked first you had to yield — so no one looked. So I moved from being a very comfortable driver, to extremely uncomfortable. Why? I was not familiar with the situation at all.

The point is, anything we do that is unfamiliar is uncomfortable. It is change, and we typically do not like change. As adults, it makes us feel inadequate. We do not like feeling inadequate. Push through this feeling. It will be worth the effort. I promise.

One Book — 2 Peter

This study is the basis for what I have been doing with my sons for the past four years. John (my oldest) and I have finished all 66 books. Jeff (my middle son) and Brian (my youngest) have been in and out of the study because of college and work schedules. This is also the method that I cover in our workshops. In the interest of full disclosure here, Psalms and Proverbs do not lend themselves easily to this study. I'll have more on that at the end of this section.

What we have been doing is meeting at a restaurant once a week, having already completed the study. We then compare notes and talk about what we have learned.

What this is not

Possibly more important than what this is, may be what this is not. This study[1] is not intended to be an attempt to get it "right" — this is an overview. The focus is like the first step of the chapter analysis, to get a bird's eye view of the book. Secondly, to see how the message of the book fits into the overall flow of the Bible. We are striving to see the contribution each book of the Bible makes in relationship to the overall purpose of the Bible and our knowledge of God (i.e., see parts in relationship to the whole).

Study Concepts

1. Forest for trees — this is an overview. To paraphrase Dave Jewitt, "If you are analytic, get over that for this study." You are trying to get the big picture here.

2. See it from on high — about 50,000 feet. Read fast. Skim. Resist the pull to really dive into one verse.

3. "Un"detail (don't get bogged down in the details.) Are you getting the message yet? We are not interested in verb tenses or parts of speech. How does the book as a whole hang together? What are the big chunks?

---

[1] The study method is a modified synthetic overview of a book this has come from several sources. First, a Bible study that was led by Harry Steck in 1973; second, a series of tapes by Howard Hendricks used by Terry Cook in a Bible study at the University of Alabama in 1975. The idea of using this in an overview of the New Testament came from a summer training program led by Larry Whitehouse in 1978. The final form and notion of using this as an overview of the Bible with your sons came from a request by my son, John, two years ago. Finally, the idea of sharing this with men in a seminar came from conversations with Brent Lollis, Nathan Baxter, and Dave Jewitt. So if you do the math this has taken thirty-seven years to develop.

4. Don't look for "right understanding," look for familiarization. This may be the hardest one. You are trying to get familiar with the book. You are trying to get to the point that at the end of the study you could think your way through the content of the book in big portions.

Study Format

Read through this study completely before you start. It will give you a sense of where you are going with the study.

1. Skim the book three times at one sitting each. You already know this, but these books were written without chapter and verses. The epistles are letters. For the most part, each book of the Bible was intended to be read in one sitting. Most of the epistles can be read in less than an hour. Some much more quickly than that. Resist the pull to slow down. As stated above, you are trying to familiarize yourself with the book. Think of it this way. When you are reading through a book and do not understand the overall argument, you try to figure it out as you read the parts. The purpose of skimming and this overview is to get a handle on the flow of the book so that when you do come back for analysis you understand better the context of the sections you are analyzing.

   As you skim through the book, it helps to be looking for specific information. If you have a study Bible that has an introduction to the book, please do not read it at this point. Work through this yourself first. Then compare your answers to the introduction.

1.1. Reading one — I repeat, read it fast. A book like 2 Peter should not take more than 15 – 20 minutes to skim. As you skim through the book the first time look for:

1.1.1. <u>What is the historical background?</u>

    1.1.1.1. <u>By whom written</u> — For most of the New Testament this is obvious. But look for specific verses that reveal this to you.

    1.1.1.2. <u>To whom written</u> — For the epistles this is also somewhat easy; one can usually tell by the title or the content. In the Old Testament this can be a bit trickier. If you have a concordance, look for names that show up in the text. Where those names appear in other books may give you a clue as to whom the book was written.

    1.1.1.3 <u>When and where written</u> — For Paul's epistles, reviewing the three missionary journeys can guide you on when and where he was when he wrote the letters. The recipients of Paul's letters are fairly obvious. For other books, look at the content for clues.

1.1.2. <u>What are the recurring words and phrases?</u> Remember to look for repetition, as I mentioned throughout this book. It is a great way to find the main point the author is making. It is a little like the teachers you used to have that would stomp their feet in front of the class to let you know that something was going to be on the test.

1.1.3. <u>What are the recurring themes?</u> This is beyond repetition of words or phrases. It deals with ideas that may be presented in different ways in the book. Words that are repeated may give you a clue. For example the word *entrust* shows up in 1 and 2 Timothy. The sequence describes the entrusting of the ministry of the Gospel to Paul, his subsequently entrusting it to Timothy, and Paul's charge for Timothy to entrust it to faithful men who will in turn entrust the ministry of the Gospel to others. This is much more than evangelism; it is the multiplication of laborers for the harvest. The theme is picked up by observing the repetition of the term in both of the epistles.

Set your study aside for a day or so to allow your subconscious to work on it.

1.2. Reading two — Still you are simply skimming the book. This time you are looking for:

1.2.1. <u>Your impressions of the author's style</u> - Fast-moving, dramatic, casual, flowing, heavy teaching, narrative, etc. Write down your impressions in a couple of sentences.

1.2.2. <u>Atmosphere of the book</u> - How do you feel after you read it? Challenged, blessed, motivated, etc.? Record your feelings in a couple of sentences as well.

1.2.3. <u>Key passages</u> — Notice passages that jump out to you as you are skimming the book, passages that make you want to slow down, or passages that especially speak to what is going on in your life. Also, look for sections that seem to capture the central ideas of the book.

1.2.4. <u>Divisions/Tentative outline</u> — The last thing you want to do on this reading is to look for how you may want to divide the book. The idea here is to enable yourself to think through the content of the book. What are the chunks that seem to fit best together? Make a note of the start and end verses and the main thought for each division. You will validate this in the next reading.

Again, set this aside for a day or two and then come back. All right, I know that I have said in other places to soak yourself in the text. We will explain that process later on.

1.3. Reading three — You will skim the book one more time. This time through you are looking for:

1.3.1. <u>Main theme</u> — Capture what you think the main theme of the book is in five words or less. What verses led you to that conclusion?

1.3.2. <u>How the theme is developed</u> — How does the author develop his argument? Is it logical, does he use examples and narrative, does he refer to other works? What are the main literary devices he uses to get his point across?

    1.3.3. <u>Finalize your divisions/outline</u> — In reading two, you identified tentative divisions and an outline. This time, read through with your outline in mind and make any changes you feel are needed.

2. Prepare a simple outline or chart of the book, give a unique title to the book, and select the key verse or passage. Being visual I prefer charts to outlines. The appendix has a guide on how to do a simple chart.

3. Application: As we have covered before, this is really the most important part of the study. Refer to the application section under Verse Analysis and Chapter Analysis below for details on how to develop an application.

4. Optional: These are questions that you may want to dive into if you have extra time. Sometimes I use these questions to stimulate the conversation with my sons as we are discussing a book at our breakfast meetings.

    4.1. Develop in basic statement or outline form an answer to the following question: What does this book uniquely emphasize about Jesus Christ? (His Person and His work — or what would we not understand about God and/or the Christian life if we did not have this book?)

    4.2. What intrigues you about this book? What would you like to study again later in more depth?

    4.3. What situation would draw you back to this book for answers?

4.4. What one or two main topics of Christian living are uniquely emphasized in this book? What is the lesson on that topic?

4.5. Look up key people in a concordance and/or a dictionary. What is their role in the book?

4.6. Look up areas and cities mentioned in a Bible atlas or dictionary. What is their significance to the overall message?

4.7. Identify and describe in one or two sentences any problems addressed in the book.

Guidelines

While working through this study with my boys, we allowed ourselves six hours to complete a long book like one of the Gospels or Romans. In all honesty, Isaiah took us about eight weeks to finish. There were school issues and travel issues with that book; plus it is extremely long and complex.

For a small book like Philippians, we allowed three hours. That was and is adequate.

Throughout the New Testament, we found that doing a long book, followed by a short book worked better. For example, a Gospel followed by a short epistle like 1 Peter.

For the Old Testament, we studied chronologically through to Nehemiah. After that we mostly followed the same approach, long books alternating with short, through the rest of the Old Testament. There are many more long books than short in the Old Testament. Allow yourself some grace if it takes you more than a week or two to do some of the books. As I mentioned earlier, it took us eight to get through Isaiah. Balance your need to take more time with the fact that you are doing an overview here. Don't fall into the trap of letting every book you do stretch over into multiple weeks.

We have found that Psalms and Proverbs do not lend themselves to this type of study.

Proverbs

We approached Proverbs topically, as follows:

1. Read through Proverbs, and pick out all verses that apply to a specific topic, character trait, or issue. One example is the tongue.

2. Group the verses into topics as follows:

    2.1. Descriptive

    2.2. Benefits

    2.3. Detriments

    2.4. Commandments

    2.5. Miscellaneous

3. Locate a key verse for each topic.

4. Write out a central teaching on the topic, using Proverbs only.

5. Write out an application.

Psalms

For Psalms, we started by attempting to tackle the 150 Psalms in five separate book divisions:

Book 1	1 – 41
Book 2	42 – 72
Book 3	73 – 89
Book 4	90 – 106
Book 5	107 – 150

We attempted to do one book section at a time, but this did not work. I think we made it through Book 2.

Now we are studying ten Psalms at a time alongside another study we are doing. We found that it is hard to do a lot of Psalms at once. We typically try to come up with:

1. A title for the Psalm.

2. Divisions, if there are any that make sense.

3. A key verse.

4. An application from the group of ten we are doing.

So that is it. You can work your way through the Bible using this method. As I mentioned earlier, John and I have finished all sixty-six books. It has given him a grasp of the overall story of redemption. Jeff and Brian have a personal handle on the books that they have done.

For the next study, I am going to suggest the one that I started with — verse analysis. I have found that this study is like a foundational brick. From it you can build to just about any in-depth study, verse, chapter, book, or topic. If you first learn to study one verse, and then learn how the verses fit together, you can master any section of scripture.

I suggest you start with a verse you know very well.

One Verse — John 15:5

"I am the vine, you are the branches; he who abides in Me and I in him, he bears much fruit, for apart from Me you can do nothing."[2]

If you have been in the Christian community very long, you have heard a sermon on this verse. You may have heard more than one, and you may have it memorized. You may have even studied the verse in the context of another Bible study. It is packed.

The following are eight steps that will give you the tools to unpack this or any other verse.

As I mentioned the first time I did this, I invested three hours in the study. That is not a requirement or an expectation. You can spend three minutes, thirty minutes, three hours, or more. Obviously, the more time you invest, the greater the return.

Why not get a sheet of paper and your Bible and try this now?

First, ask the Lord to lead you and show you what He wants you to see through this study. Then:

1. <u>Determine the thought preceding the verse</u>. Try to capture the main idea in a single paragraph. Indicate the references which you feel incorporate this thought. How far back you read is up to you. You are trying to get a sense of the context of the verse you are considering.

---

[2] If you have the companion workbook, there is space for you to do this study. I have also put my personal study in there so you can compare your answers with mine. What I have is not an answer key, but rather a point of comparison to give you encouragement that you are on the right track. You may not see exactly the same things that I do in the verse, but that is a function of gifts and experience. I am certain that if I could see your study, I would learn things from you. Such is the nature of the body of Christ.

2. <u>Read the verses immediately following</u>. What is the thought following the verse? Follow the same pattern as you did in step 1. Again, how far you read is up to you.

3. <u>Look up key words</u> in the verse in a standard dictionary, and list definitions that illuminate the meaning of the verse. Definitions drawn from a Bible dictionary may also be very useful. Note here that the older dictionary you can find the better. Newer dictionaries tend to be politically correct, but the older dictionaries may actually reference the Bible.

This can be one of the richest parts of your study. Look up words that you think you know. I have found that doing so forces me to consider shades of meaning of the verse that I may not have considered otherwise.

4. <u>Consider the pertinent statements of fact</u> in the verse. This is asking the question, "What does this say?" (Observation)

The following questions may help your observation:

4.1. The six W's

4.1.1. Who — who does the verse talk about or who is being addressed?

4.1.2. Where — where is the passage written to or from; is there anything about this that helps you understand the thought of the verse?

4.1.3. What — what is being said? Do not ask here what is meant, which is the interpretation question. Stay with observation, what is actually being said.

4.1.4. Why — why is this here? How does it relate to the verses you looked at before and after the text?

4.1.5. When — this can go a couple of different ways. How does the statement in the verse fit in chronologically with the Bible; when does it happen in the story? Second, if there is a command or suggestion, is there a timeframe or sequence with which it is associated?

4.1.6. Wherefore — or so what? What is the action this passage requires?

4.2. Other general helps. This could feel a bit like high school English, but trust me it will help you. During a Bible study we had at a university, the students were struggling with one of Paul's sentences. In order to help them sort it out, I asked them to identify the subject of the sentence. After an awkward pause, I changed the question and had them identify nouns in the sentence. Shortly after that session, I found myself teaching English grammar in the study.

The Bible was written with vocabulary and grammar. Some of the richest observations can come from noticing how the Holy Spirit used these tools to communicate with us.

Do not get hung up on this and feel overwhelmed; just do what you can. Bite off a little at a time, and you will be surprised how quickly this comes back. I was no model student through high school and college. I graduated from A&M with a 2.0 GPA, the bare minimum. When I started studying the Bible, the incredible richness and depth of the text drew me in like a parched deer to the water. But I was frustrated that I did not understand how the sentences were structured. One of the members of the church I was attending gave me a book on sentence diagramming.[3] I worked through it and essentially relearned grammar (I still cannot spell). It has greatly enhanced the quality of the observations I am able to make. But, if this is a struggle for you, do not dwell here. You will still get much out of the study even if you skip this section. I encourage you, if you are interested in increasing your skill and the skill of your children, this is worth whatever time you choose to invest.

4.2.1. Note verbs used. One of the reasons for this is the heavy dependence on verbs in Greek and Hebrew to communicate the author's thoughts.

4.2.2. Note adjectives and adverbs. They qualify and expand the words they modify. This is where you will find shades of meaning.

4.2.3. Does the word order have any special significance?

4.2.4. Are there significant contrasts, comparisons, or repetitions in ideas, phrases, or people? This is a key question and the beginning of looking at logical structure.[4]

---

[3] Emery, Donald W. *Sentence Analysis.* Holt, Rinehart, and Winston: New York, 1961.

[4] In the annotated bibliography you will find a book by Robert Traina, *Methodical Bible Study.* This book is a seminal work on Bible study methods. It is very difficult to read, but it has a wealth of information about how to use structure to unlock the riches of the Bible. I highly recommend it, but you may have to stand up to read it.

4.2.5. If people are mentioned, what do you know about them that helps your understanding?

5. Select cross references that:

    5.1. Answer questions.

    5.2. Illustrate.

    5.3. Clarify or expand the thought.

    5.4. Possibly contradict.

6. Outline or diagram the verse (if possible) and explain the thought of the verse. Draw upon your context (thoughts before and after), definitions, observations, and cross-references to fully expound the meaning of the verse. This is pulling together all of your observations into a summary of your study.

7. Create your own paraphrase of the verse. A paraphrase is a free rendering of the sense of the passage. Try to avoid excessive amplification of the passage. Check to be sure that your paraphrase has not altered the meaning of the verse.

8. Make a written application of the verse to your own life. This is really important. Our Father did not give us His Word to make us smarter. He gave it to us to know Him through applying it. It is neither enough nor the objective of any study to become a Bible trivia expert. In John 5:39-40, Jesus, talking to the leaders of the Jews says, "You search the Scriptures because you think that in them you have eternal life; it is these that testify about Me; and you are unwilling to come to Me so that you may have life." These people had the first five books of the Bible memorized. Jesus says they do not know

Him, they do not know the Father, they do not have the love of God in them, and they are not seeking the glory of God. Obviously, knowledge of the Bible is not enough.

In contrast, Ezra 7:10 tells us, "For Ezra had set his heart to study the law of the Lord and to practice it, and to teach His statutes and ordinances in Israel." Note the sequence here: he set his heart, studied, practiced, and then taught. He practiced and applied the Word of God to his life first. Then he taught others.

In the New Testament the same thought is echoed in James 1:22: "But prove yourselves doers of the word, and not merely hearers who delude themselves." Our interaction with the Word of God will change us. If it does not, James says we are delusional.

The following questions and suggestions are listed to assist you in making a practical application:

8.1. What is the truth of the verse? (Review #6 above.)

8.2. How does this truth relate to me?

8.2.1. What part of this truth have I already embraced?

8.2.2. What part is new to me?

8.2.3. What requires a change of thought?

8.2.4. What is already a part of my action?

8.2.5. What can be immediately applied to my behavior?

8.2.6. What am I doing that is wrong?

8.2.7. What action must I take now?

8.2.8. What will I need from this that might help me in the future?

8.3. When deciding upon a course of action:

8.3.1. Keep it simple.

8.3.2. Make it practical.

8.3.3. Set a time limit.

8.3.4. Plan a check-up and reward.

That's it. You have studied a verse and applied it. I have worked through this study with numerous men. The reaction is always the same. They start the process somewhat hesitantly, wondering if it will be worth the time. All of them come back to the next meeting blown away by what they have found. Some of them already had the verse memorized, but found a depth and richness there that they had not imagined. I also did this remotely, over the phone with a guy in Florida. After he had shared the results of his study with me, he confessed that it gave him a whole new confidence in the Word of God and his ability to share it with others.

I guarantee that will be your experience as well.

The key to this study is that it slows us down. Following the eight steps allows us to read the verse as if for the first time. It prevents us from passing over things that are there in the text. Also, it forces us to remain in the first question we talked about in the last chapter, "What does it say?" As I mentioned then, if we answer that question well, the meaning of the text becomes pretty clear.

The next study we are going to look at slows you down even more. We are going to look at how to study one word.

One Word — Abundantly

John 10:10 - "The thief comes only to steal and kill and destroy; I came that they may have life, and have it **abundantly**."

Word studies bring more insight and depth to a Bible study. There can be many levels to a word study. This is a relatively simple four-step process that will yield rich results for you.

1. Look up the word in a good dictionary. Determine which definition best fits the context. Reviewing the other definitions may give you insight on how the word could be used.

    N.B.[5] *As mentioned before, the older the dictionary the better; if you can use the Oxford English Dictionary that is even better. An old unabridged dictionary is a second best option.*

2. Look up the word in a Bible dictionary, or word study guide like Wuest, Vines, or Vincent (see annotated bibliography for description of these works.)

3. Use a concordance to find other verses where the word is used.

    Note on using an English Concordance:
    Remember that an English Concordance is keyed to English words. While that is obvious, it creates some limitations for us as we study the Bible. For

---

[5] N.B. is short for a Latin phrase meaning "note well." It is used in English to draw a reader's attention to an important point. It is like when a teacher used to stomp their foot in front of class to emphasize that the point they were making was important and would be on the test.

instance, there are four Greek words that are rendered *love* in English, three of which appear in our Bible. So if you are looking up "love" in your English concordance, you will get every place that the word *love* appears in the text, however you will not know on the surface which word you are looking up in Greek. Strong's solves this by numbering the words. So if you are looking up *agape* or *love* you would scan the references in your concordance for 26. In that way, you would be looking for occurrences of *agape* rather than *phileo* or *eros*. If you have access to an *Englishman's Greek Concordance* or *The Word Study Concordance,* these works are based on the Greek and will give you a list of all the verses in which the actual Greek root word you are investigating appears.

These next steps, you will notice, are like concentric circles.

3.1. Look for other places the word is used in the book which contains the verse you are studying. In the case of John 10:10, does John use this word elsewhere in the Gospel of John, and if so, how?

3.2. Study how the author of the book uses the word in other books, if any, that he wrote. Compare how he uses the word in other places. For this verse you would look to see if John used "abundantly" in 1, 2, or 3 John, or Revelation.

3.3. Look for how other authors use the word.

4. Summarize your observations.

While these studies can be time consuming, they add a greater understanding to your study that you can only appreciate after you do one. They really slow us down to consider the real meaning, and in step three, they move us to look throughout the Bible into how the themes associated with the word we are studying are developed. That can quickly expose you to a cross-section of how the various human authors of the Bible treat a specific topic.

We slowed down to study a verse and a word, so now let's pick up the pace a bit and look at how to study a chapter at a time.

One Chapter — 1 John 1

The next study we will consider is chapter analysis. Chapter analysis uses and builds on the skill we developed in verse analysis and word studies. The goal of chapter analysis is to wring the text dry, to get as much as possible out of our time with the Bible. To do this we will use all of the four questions we mentioned in Chapter 2:

- What does it say? (Observation)

- What does it mean? (Interpretation)

- What does it say in other places? (Correlation)

- What does it say that I need to do? (Application)

The most important step to our understanding the text is observation. So, we will focus on increasing observational skills in this study.

This is a four-step study. We will move from the whole — the chapter to the parts — the verses and terms used by John and back to the whole. So we look at the chapter as an overview, take it apart, and then put it back together again. The fourth step is to apply what we have learned to our lives. Again, this may seem daunting, but the more you do it the more it will become second nature. So the study looks like:

1. Chapter Overview

2. Verse-by-Verse Analysis

3. Chapter Summary

4. Application

There is more than one way to study a chapter. You can follow what we do here and modify it, or you can look at some of the resources listed in the annotated bibliography and follow those procedures. They all have similar elements. Before you start, read through all of the steps. Not all of them will apply to 1 John 1; they are listed here for your use as you study other chapters.

You may want to mark up the text as you are reading. If you are like me and don't want to mark up your Bible, there is another option. Typically, I do my Bible study in Microsoft Word. That way I can underline, highlight, or make bold — whatever I want — without marking up my Bible. If you would like to do that with this study, you can download a word version of 1 John 1 set up for this Bible study. To download the file type http://entrust-ingtruth.org/index.cfm?id=68 in the address field of your browser. Click on the link for 1 John 1 on the page, and the file will download to your computer. You should save it somewhere you will remember, like your desktop.

First John 1 contains only ten verses, but they are packed. If you follow these steps, you will unlock truths within that you have not seen before. I promise.

So let's get started.

1. <u>Chapter Overview</u>. Read through the chapter several times, at least once a day. If possible read it several times a day. If you have a PDA and can load a copy on it, do that. If you downloaded the chapter from the website, print it and take it with you wherever you go. When you stop for coffee or are on a break, read it again. If you are waiting for an appointment, are between tasks, are on a bathroom break (it is OK to read the Bible in there), or riding an elevator, pull it out and read through it. These are examples of what Paul talks about in Ephesians 5:16, "making the most of your time." Most chapters can be read in just a few minutes; this one in about two. The idea is to immerse yourself in the text. Read it over and over until you almost know it by heart.

One word of encouragement here. If you are doing this with a group, do not wait until the night before to start your study. Bible study is a lot like barbeque. What? OK, it is like preparing the meat for barbeque. The longer you marinate the meat, the better the result. In this case, the meat is your heart and mind and the marinade is the Word of God. Work on this throughout the week and allow your subconscious mind the opportunity to soak in what you are studying.

1.1. While you are reading the chapter look for:

    1.1.1. Repetition — Repetition is one of the best ways to note what the author is saying. As you read through the text, note what is repeated. Highlight or underline in your Bible, on your photocopied page, or the MS Word document the elements that are repeated. Some things to look for:

        1.1.1.1. Words — are there words that are repeated in the chapter? Include synonyms or verbal forms of nouns.

        1.1.1.2. Phrases — does the author use a phrase repeatedly, use similar phrases, or use the same phrase rearranged?

    1.1.2. Structure — You may have heard it said, "If you see a 'therefore' in the Bible, you have to see what it is there for." That is because "therefore" is a structural marker. It usually means that whatever comes before the "therefore" causes or results in what comes after the "therefore". "Therefore" is not the only word that gives us clues like this. Here are some words you may see in 1 John 1 and what they may indicate for you:

Words	May indicate
from	temporal or location
so that, in order that	purpose
indeed	emphatic
if	condition
but, although, yet	contrast
as, or, so, also, just as, so also, like	comparison
for, because	reason

As you encounter these words in the text, circle, underline, or highlight them. Look for patterns like strings of conditional statements or contrasts. Looking for these patterns can be extremely helpful in understanding the overall argument of the author in the section you are studying.

Note: In this section of the study, resist trying to answer questions. You are reading to get a handle on the chapter as a whole. As you work through the section verse by verse, you will benefit from having looked at the chapter as a whole, and you will have a better feel for how each element relates to the whole.

1.2. Pepper the text with questions. The questions here should be at the chapter level. What intrigues you about the unit as a whole? What are the implications?

1.3. Look for terms that you do not understand. Highlight or circle them. Do not try to define them now, we will do that as we go through the passage verse by verse.

1.4. Notice the pace and rhythm of the text. Is it quick or slow? Is the information detailed or is it more of an overview? Does John write in long thoughts or short bursts? This type of observation can help you to see divisions in the text as well as changes in purpose.

1.5. Look for how you might outline the chapter. At this point, you are looking for major sections, not details.

2. <u>Verse By Verse Analysis</u>. Here, we study how each verse advances, amplifies, or clarifies the theme or message of the chapter. Read verse by verse through the chapter, making detailed observations on each verse. If you use the Microsoft Word document from the website, you can type your observations in the right column. Or you could, like I did before I started doing Bible study on my computer, turn a piece of paper sideways (landscape), draw a line down the middle of the page, and write the verse you are studying on the left and your observations on the right.

However you choose to do this, make sure that you write down your observations. As we mentioned when we were looking at verse analysis, the benefit and purpose of this process is to slow you down as you study the text.

Essentially, what you are doing here is the observation portion (steps three through five) of the verse analysis study for each verse. You will find yourself picking and choosing which of the steps to do on each verse. The key verses will draw you further in. Do not force this; have fun with it. The more you study, the more efficient you will become in picking which verses to investigate more deeply.

2.1. In addition to the questions in the verse analysis study, you may want to consider the following:

2.1.1. When a term is repeated, is it always used in the same way? If not, what does that tell you? If it is, what does that suggest?

2.1.2. As you are reading through the passage, are there terms that you wonder about, either in meaning or usage? If so, make a note of them and look them up in a standard dictionary, or better yet, a Bible dictionary.

2.1.3. Jot down questions you have about the chapter or any of the sections. Do not worry about answering them now. You may find that as you ask questions, others come to mind. Make a note of those as well. If you begin to formulate answers to the questions as you ask them, and they seem to fit the text, make a note of them.

2.1.4. Pay attention to the verbs that are being used. What do they tell you about the message? Look at the verbs used here, how would you characterize them, as statements, commands, or something else? What does John's verb use tell you about the chapter?

2.1.5. Analyze key words or terms you have identified that warrant a more in-depth study; perhaps because you need a better definition. Use the process discussed earlier.

2.1.6. Cross references. One way for better understanding of what is meant by a phrase or term is to see how the author or other authors in the Bible have dealt with the topic or term. If your Bible has cross references, see where else John refers to a term in which you are interested. If you do not have cross references you can look up the word in a concordance. Or, if you do not have a concordance, you can use Bible Gateway's word search function, type http://www.biblegateway.com/keyword/ in your browser address and enter your word in the search field. You can limit the search in the options section to include only John's writings (you will have to enter them one at a time — John, 1 John, 2 John, 3 John, Revelation) for the first part of your study and then expand to the other authors in subsequent searches. That is one way to work through the phases of how a word is used by the author, the author in other books, and other authors, as we talked about when we examined word studies earlier.

Another way to find cross references is to use a topical Bible. Nave's is the one that is most readily available. If you do not have access to Nave's, you can use the Bible Gateway topical search function. type http://www.biblegateway.com/topical/ in your browser address and enter the topic for which you would like to find references.

How does what you find in these passages affect your understanding of John's message here?

3. <u>Chapter Summary</u>. This is where we pull back together all that we learned from the study, and it's an integral step. You are reassembling everything you have taken apart as you worked through the passage. It is so important because it reinforces what you have learned.

3.1. Look over your verse — by verse analysis.

3.1.1. How would you describe the main point of the chapter? Write this out as completely as you can.

3.1.2. What do the repetitions in the chapter, if any, tell you about the theme?

3.1.3. This was written for a purpose. How would you describe the purpose based on your study?

3.1.4. What questions do you have that are still not answered? It is OK to have unanswered questions. But keep track of them. Later studies may shed light on questions from this study.

3.2. Outline or chart the chapter.[5] Develop a top-level outline of the chapter down to paragraphs or the major sections.

3.2.1. Create a title for each section of the chapter, but not more than five words. It should be unique and help you remember clearly the content. Strive to have a title that will force you back to this passage. Something that you cannot confuse with another portion of scripture. To do this step well is difficult, but worth the effort because it will drive home the content deep into your memory bank.

3.2.2. Write a five-word title for the chapter. If you were to summarize the message of this chapter into one short five-word sentence, what would that sentence be? (It may take you several attempts to pinpoint the essence of what you have studied.)

---

[6] There are examples of charts and outlines on the website on the same page the Word file for 1 John 1 was found.

3.2.3. Pick a key verse. Which verse in this chapter best captures the thought you expressed in your five-word title. Again, think this through. The more effort you put into this, the stronger your grasp of the content will become.

4. <u>Application</u>. Follow the same pattern we covered in the verse analysis study.

Some other questions or things to consider:

4.1. The way we respond to the Bible is data in our study, just as the way we respond to people is data in our relationship with them. What does your response to John's ideas tell you about yourself, or about how God might be working in you right now?

4.1.1. Is there something that challenges you in this chapter? If so, what is it? Pray about where the Lord may be taking you with that challenge.

4.1.2. Are there some difficult suggestions? How do you find yourself responding to those suggestions? As you pray through your response, what do you sense the Lord is directing you to do? Take time to reflect and write on this.

4.2. Consider memorizing the verse that you chose to represent the content of the chapter.

4.3. What are the key things that you have learned from the chapter?

4.4. What questions have been raised for you during this study? What has changed in your relationship to the Word of God?

4.5. What about this chapter challenges you? What can you do differently?

And now, you are done.

- So let's take stock of where we are. If you have worked through this with me, you can now analyze a verse of scripture, dig deep into the meaning of a critical word, analyze a book, and synthesize a chapter. With these building blocks, there is little that you cannot do in the Word of God. You can incorporate the skills you have learned to continue investigating the Bible at many levels. For example: You can do a topical study, which is essentially a word study that looks at what the Bible as a whole says about a word.

- You can study a book by doing an overview, then a chapter analysis on each chapter or section if you choose not to divide the book at the chapters. Then you can synthesize your study by using the overview study to summarize your work.

Where to Study

My sons and I have met in restaurants. It gets us away from the house to a place where we won't be interrupted and makes it special. We ate at the same table long enough at one restaurant that the waitress knew what we wanted to eat. Lasting memories were created. When the boys drive by that place, they will always remember our time together studying the Bible.

I highly recommend that you find a place where you can meet together that will create a similar memory.

Those are the core studies. That is what we have done and what we are doing. Jump in.

Now that you know what to do, how do you get your kids involved?

CHAPTER 5
Involving Your Kids

OK, we have worked on ourselves. We have the bricks for building. But the whole point of this book is to build the truth of scripture into the lives of our kids. How?

John, our oldest child, is gifted. I know that all parents believe their kid is smart, but John really is. He tested in the 99.9 percentile in every test administered to him. He was born in Knoxville when we were on the staff of the Navigators at the University of Tennessee. We lived in the West part of the city in a hilly neighborhood. We had a really steep driveway that came down to our house, which sat about halfway down the hill. The sidewalk to the front door came off of the porch, and then did a ninety degree turn to the driveway. The garage was on the side of the house, and there was a paved area in front of the garage big enough for two or three cars to park.

John was neither tall nor strong enough at the time to pedal his tricycle. Actually, it was my old trike we had refinished for him. I would set him on the trike and push him around the driveway, the garage, the parking area in front of the garage, and up the sidewalk to the front door with a pole that I had notched to fit on the platform on the back of the tricycle.

To teach him to steer, I told him to point the tire in the direction he wanted to go. At that point he leaned over the handlebars, extended his right arm completely, and pointed his index finger at the tire. It was all I could do to stay standing as I was laughing so hard.

This past summer we finished an overview of the Bible together that I described in Chapter Four. John wanted to go deeper into Romans. So we were going through the book using chapter analysis (also Chapter Four) one chapter at a time. Monday morning, John and I were in Romans 7. We were talking about the nature of sin, discussing when it was that Adam sinned and whether sin was an action or a state of being. We were also delving into the relationship between the law and sin trying to determine in what sense sin was dead prior to the introduction of the law. He has come a long way from pointing the tire.

I am not sure how many dads get to do what I did with John on Monday. We did not get there by starting the week before. He was about 18 months old when he pointed the tire, he is 28 now. So about...26.5 years? We have done a number of things with him and his sister and brothers to get to this point. None of it was hard. Not all of it worked. We just kept at it.

Later this year, John and his wife, Morgan, are presenting us with our first grandchild. One really great thing for us is that we know this process will continue. John is already planning how he can get their child into the Word early.

Start when they are young.

Before we go much further, I want to make sure that you understand what is being shared here. These are all of the things that I can remember that we tried. The key word is tried. Some ideas worked better than others. Some we should have continued longer and could have implemented better than we did. They are shared here to do two things. First, to give you some ideas; you may and should modify these to fit your children and your situation. They may spark some new ideas for you. Great.

Second, to let you know that it is a continual learning process. There is no magic formula to this challenge. You just pray and keep trying.

Infant and Pre School

Read

We literally started before our kids were born. Obviously, this was by praying for them. When Jenny had her quiet times, she would read her Bible out loud. It is not clear in the research whether children can hear or how well they can hear in utero, but Jenny read out loud. If nothing more, it was our way of committing to starting the process of exposing our children to the Word. It got us in the habit of involving our kids in the Word. So when you have your quiet time, read aloud to your child. It is bonding, and it is good for them to hear your voice.

Toys

There are a number of toys now with biblical themes. We had a Noah's ark that had animals that went through shaped holes in the ark and were different colors. So in addition to fine motor skills, color recognition, and pattern matching, we were able to talk about a Bible story. A little time on the Internet or in your local Christian bookstore will give you a lot of great ideas.

Fun

One of the keys to success with young children is to make this fun. Make it a game. Build the wall of Jericho with blocks, and then march around it seven times blowing horns and knock down the blocks. Tell the Bible stories and act them out with toys. Keep it light. But keep it consistent.

Books

We had a couple of really good colorful books, *Read-Aloud Bible Stories*[1] we had Volumes 1, 2, and 3; Volume 4 is now available. These books are great on several levels. They have really good colorful pictures. The stories are condensed and translated into words that a child can grasp. We would read and re-read them with our children. Each time through we would ask them what the pictures were about and read the words out loud. So they were getting exposed not only to Bible stories, but to reading as well.

Games

This goes along with fun. Make your time with the kids in and around the Word fun by playing games. We played with the toy Noah's ark with the kids and talked to them about the story as we put the animals on the boat two by two. That is fun at bath time.

---

[1] Ella K. Lindvall, *Read Aloud Bible Stories, Vol. 1,* (Chicago: Moody Press, 1982). Volumes 2, 3, and 4 are the same publisher 1985, 1990, and 1995 respectively. These books are available on my website.

Songs and Media

We sang a bunch of songs with our kids that had catchy tunes and biblical content. They are available at most Christian book stores. I play guitar, so I would play and the whole family would sing with me. If you do not play an instrument, you can use the CD player.

We also had some videos by Tyndale House, "McGee and Me." They were well done and had biblical messages. I have not seen Veggie Tales, but have heard really good things about them. The point is, there are resources available on DVD that are well made and have biblical content. You can watch them with your child — that is key — watch it with them and then talk about what you have seen.

Catechism

When John was about two, we started working with him in the Catechism for Young Children[2] This is a scaled down version of the Westminster Catechism. As he was young, we worked on the questions that had short answers that a child his age could handle. We also filtered out the questions that had answers that we were not comfortable with, for either biblical or theological reasons. The reason I say that is not to criticize the catechism, but rather to underscore that the responsibility of what my children learned was Jenny's and mine, not those who published the

---

[2] I have looked for a source for this booklet and have not been able to find one. I did find the questions on a website and have created a document that has all of the questions for your use. You can find this on the website page on which you found the 1 John 1 file (http://entrustingtruth.org/index. cfm?id = 68).

works. If I had questions about the content, I did not teach it to John. You should feel that same freedom. Bottom line, while he was very young we focused on questions 1 – 20 of the catechism. He learned all of them.

My office was in the basement of our home in Knoxville. We had a larger room just outside my office where we held meetings. There was a piano in that room for practice and sing-alongs. John was playing with one of his cars on the piano bench one afternoon where I could hear him. Questions six through eight of the catechism are:

Q. 6. Are there more gods than one?
A. There is only one God.

Q. 7. In how many persons does this one God exist?
A. In three persons.

Q. 8. What are they?
A. The Father, the Son, and the Holy Ghost.

As John was moving his car across various parts of the piano, he was saying to himself over and over, "The Father, the Son, and the Holy Goose." Close. Since our last name of Cunningham is Scottish, and the Scots call the Holy Spirit the Wild Goose, I was OK with John's edit.

One thing to mention is that our kids were all different. When it was time to begin with Ranae, she had a different idea. We suggested working through the questions, and she looked at us with a look that said, "Why in the world would I want to do that? That does not seem like fun." That was pretty much the end of that. We worked with her for several weeks, but it was not her thing.

We did not try with Jeff and Brian. Our life circumstances changed radically around Jeff's birth, and we did not adjust as quickly as we should have.

Ranae did enjoy the next thing we tried....

Crayon Bible Study

This is something that we did with John and Ranae. We were outnumbered with Jeff and Brian and did not attempt this with them.

I would bring John and Ranae into my office separately. I would give them a blank piece of paper and a box of crayons. I would then read a verse of scripture to them. We started in Genesis 1, the story of creation. After I read the passage, I would ask them to tell me what the verse was saying. For Genesis 1:1-2, John said that was "the mess." So I asked him to draw me a picture of "the mess." He did that, and then we labeled the sheet Genesis 1:1-2 on the top of the page. Then I had him create a cover for the binder that would hold his pictures. We punched the sheet and put it in the binder. The binder went on the shelf in my office with the rest of my books. It was important. I did the same thing with Ranae.

The next day we would start the study by reviewing the drawings and what they meant. For instance, I would turn to John's drawing of Genesis 1:1-2 and ask him what it was. "That's the mess." We would do that for all of the pictures they had done up to that time. Then we would do the next verse.

It was fun on a lot of levels, and it got both of them involved in thinking about what scripture said and recording what they had imagined at an early age.

Elementary

You may have noticed that when kids start school, life gets more complicated. Sports, church, music, and dance lessons. We limited our kids to one sport each, church, piano lessons, and band, starting in the sixth grade. We counted about sixty-eight trips a week between 3:30 and 8:00 P.M. before John started driving. That is a lot of miles on a minivan.

So we had to adjust our plan to fit our new schedule. With four kids in elementary and preschool and me in seminary, life was a bit hectic.

Sing and Read

We continued the singing and added reading. The process was to sing a song or two, and then read a Bible story and talk about it.

AWANA

The church we were attending had AWANA. We had all of the children, with the exception of Brian who was too young at the time, in this program. We worked with them daily on their verses and other activities.

Saturday Morning Breakfast

As I have interacted with fathers over the past two years about how to engage with their children, we have come up with a modified approach to what I do now with my older sons. Rather than try to do a book or a chapter with them, do one of the following:

Verses

Take one verse and read it together, and work through a modified verse analysis with them. After one dad and I talked at lunch, I suggested these verses:

- Romans 3:23
- Romans 6:23
- Romans 5:8
- Romans 10:9-10

You may recognize this as the Roman Road. It is a clear review of the Gospel, which you and your child can go through together. It can open up conversations on salvation and how to share with their friends.

- John 15:5
- Luke 2:52
- I Timothy 4:12
- Romans 12:14-21

These verses focus on our need to continually grow in Christ. John 15 is packed; the rest center on growing as a young person.

That is eight weeks worth of breakfasts. After that you can either choose other key verses from the Bible or...

Topics

...you could cover some topics that you want to start talking about with your children. Use Nave's or the link at Bible Gateway to come up with the verses. Some ideas:

- Sharing
- Giving
- Kindness
- Serving

Character studies are essentially topical studies about a person. These would make a great conversation as well. Read portions about the person's life and talk about what makes them remarkable and what we can learn from them. People like:

- David
- Daniel and his friends
- Ruth
- Noah
- Paul
- Timothy
- Hannah
- Esther
- Gideon

There is a wealth of choices here. You can pick any name in the Old Testament and discuss with your child what they can learn from them.

The other thing you should be doing with children of this age is...

Read

Read to them. Read Bible stories. Read books for children from Christian authors. The time invested will be valuable not only spiritually, but also psychologically and academically.

Middle School

Middle school is the pits. Adolescent children can be a real chore and incredibly mean. This phase is the beginning of puberty for some, which creates hormonal storms and portends of the great times ahead in high school.

At some point during this time, you may become extremely dumb. Don't worry, you will get smarter when your child turns around 21 or 22. The key at this point is to be faithful to try to stay engaged. You will encounter a lot of rolling of eyes and deep sighs of exasperation during these years. Do not take it personally; you might want to keep a score chart of the eye rolls and sighs on an Excel spreadsheet. Maybe if you make it a game, it might be easier to endure.

It will be easier to stay engaged if you have been doing this all along from childhood. Additionally, this is a great time to be involved in a church with a strong youth program. It does not transfer the responsibility to the church, but it does help to have strong allies.

Your relationship will be changing with your children. You need to listen more now, and draw their thinking out as you are interacting over the Word. Resist preaching or talking a lot, and practice listening more. It may be difficult. In order to have your children learn to think independently, you have to allow them some rope to make mistakes.

Topics for this time will be crucial. At a father and sons weekend retreat, the men came up with topics they wanted to cover with their sons. Sexual purity topped the list. There will be others, but at this time you are beginning to build a foundation for independence. You may consider helping them learn how to do the verse analysis study.

High School

Your ability to work with your high school son or daughter will depend a great deal on their schedule and yours. If they are in extracurricular activities, it is tricky to schedule the time. My kids were all in band. In addition, Jeff was in soccer, and John was in choir, DECA, and student council. All of them were involved in the youth group and went to FCA or Young Life. John, Jeff, and Ranae were involved with Chrysalis while in high school. Their schedules were pretty full. Our role moved more toward a resource and counselor to them rather than meeting at regular times together.

When John graduated from college and we started meeting consistently, Brian was still in high school; he could not meet with us even though he wanted to because he had to be at the band room at 6:30 in the morning every day. So you have to choose to …

Be Available

You may have to change your schedule to be able to mesh with theirs. Since all our kids were in band, we got involved in the booster club. Jenny and I chaperoned band trips, and I became an officer of the club. For about 12 years, I spent a lot of time on busses with the band. Not my favorite thing, but I was available for my kids. They knew I was there even if they did not spend a lot of time with me. I also got involved with the soccer boosters and went to the games. We went to all of John's concerts and musicals. The point is we made time for what was important to them. As a result, each of them came to either one of us many times with issues with which they were dealing. We were able to talk to them about what the Bible said about their questions.

As a parent in this phase, you have to make an effort to be available and stay engaged.

Topics

If you are able to carve out regular time with them, topical studies may be the best use of your time. Issues like integrity, purity, and sharing the gospel with their peers all come to mind as things you may want to cover. These are the last years you will have significant time with them. What do you want them to leave with? Some of these may be helpful:

- Sovereignty of God
- Love of God
- Holiness of God
- Purity
- Warfare
- Walking With God
- Armor of God

You are positioning them to be independent. It is a scary, exciting time.

College

We have had four different college experiences. John and Jeff both went to the same university. They were both RA's, John was in the choir and opera; he sang the national anthem at sporting events. Jeff was in the band his freshman year until pre-med and being an RA consumed his time. Ranae started at one university and has been at four community colleges and two other universities; she is now finishing at an online university. Brian started in pre-nursing at the local community college; he lived with us for those two years. He changed to architecture and moved to one of the state universities this fall.

With the exception of the first two years with Brian, we did not have a lot of contact with them, but only through phone calls, e-mails, text messages (recently), depositing money in their bank accounts, and that type of thing. The phone calls and e-mails have been really important. While they were in three different schools, Jenny would send an email several times a week with a verse that she read during her quiet time. That was a big deal, made even bigger by the fact that she is not all that adept at computers. It took effort for her to do that; effort that included learning a skill that all of them already knew.

I received phone calls and e-mails asking about issues in the Bible and was able to respond either by e-mail or calls to talk through the issues. All of them were involved in campus Bible studies. I think the foundation was laid for that as we emphasized the importance of the Bible as described above.

John called one weekend and told me that he had a group of friends that were interested in learning how to study the Bible more effectively. Most of them were involved in Norman Young Life. I agreed to travel to Norman every other Sunday evening and walk them through the process of learning how to do a Bible study. That was an investment of about five hours on a Sunday.

It was a privilege to be able to support him in that way. Again, the foundation for that had been laid by the years we talked about the Bible before he left for school.

You may not have that option. But the principle is: stay in touch and use every opportunity you can to continue to touch their lives with the Word of God.

One word of caution, as we covered earlier. If you are not in the Word for yourself, your touches will not be as effective; they will seem forced and your son or daughter will know it.

Adult

One evening about three years ago, John called the house and told me that he had been asked to lead Sunday school at his church.

"Great!" I said.

"No, I am not ready," he replied.

I was puzzled. I have known him for a long time, and I know what he has studied in the Word. "Why?" I asked.

"I do not know how the whole Bible fits together," he explained

"Ok, so what is it you want to do?" I asked.

"Would you meet with me and take me through an overview of the Bible?" he requested.

It turns out that he had been listening to a series of messages by Howard Hendricks on Synthetic Bible Study[3] that he had down

---

[3] This is a series of eight messages titled, "Synthetic Bible Study" Prof did for the Navigator staff in the early 1970's. I was exposed to them in 1974. They have been converted to MP3 and are available at Discipleship Library.

loaded from the Discipleship Library.[4] That was the same set of messages that I had listened to on cassette tape in the mid 1970's. He asked if we could do something like that together on each book. I told him that was probably more work than he wanted to do at the time, but that I had another idea.

In the summer of '78 and '79, my wife and I were involved in a summer training program in Tallahassee and then Lexington. The program was built around an overview of the New Testament. I took that model and modified it, and we began to meet.

John and I met on Fridays at a local restaurant. The agreement was that we would do one book a week using this modified synthetic overview. The rules were that we could spend no more than three hours on a short book and six on a longer one. We alternated long and short books.

Jeff, my middle son, graduated from college shortly after we started meeting together. He was working on getting into medical school and had a year off. He joined us after we had been doing the study for a few months. Brian, the youngest, was a senior in high school when we started. Since he was in the band and they practiced in the early morning, he could not join us. In the fall when he started at the local community college, he was on board. So the four of us met weekly. I say weekly, but life happened. John had travel issues, as did I. Jeff would have pressing things to do, and Brian sometimes had to study for exams. All told, we

---

[4] http://www.discipleshiplibrary.com is a fantastic resource. There are well over 22,000 messages from hundreds of speakers. The resource is a project of the University of Oklahoma Baptist Student Union. The Navigators have contributed over 15,000 original tapes to the project. These messages are being digitized and made available on the website by topic and speaker.

probably met three out of every four weeks. Sometimes we met and one or more of us were not completely ready. That was OK. Sometimes when we came together, John would have things going on in his work, marriage, or church about which he wanted to talk. The point is that we were making progress toward our goal of getting through the Bible together, but it was not forced. We ended up meeting together with the Bible open and processing life together.

The restaurant where we met had several other groups of Christian men meeting at the same time, some from our church. One of the groups included several men who were in different positions of leadership in the church. In January of 2008, one of these men called me and asked me for more detail about what I was doing with my sons. After I told him, he asked if I could help him do the same with his sons. From that conversation grew the idea of helping fathers invest in their sons, through the workshops and this book and companion workbook.

We used the book overview described in Chapter Four. It is a low-key experience. As I mentioned above, it is a way for us to continue to touch base over the Word and process life together. There is much laughing, sometimes more laughing than Bible study. I feel privileged to be involved spiritually with my adult sons.

You may not be in the same town with your sons or daughters. That does not mean that you cannot share this with them. Using some of the webinar video tools that are available over the Internet, you can have a Bible study with someone virtually anywhere in the world and see his face. I have met with men in Florida, Virginia, and Trinidad and Tobago. It takes some getting used to, but it is doable.

A principle to remember is: do not force it. And do not turn it into an accountability deal. It is simply living life together with the Word remaining prominent in the relationship.

As I mentioned earlier, John and I have finished the sixty-six books. We are now working through Romans, step by step, using the chapter analysis described in Chapter Four. It is fun. We are struggling with some of the heavy theological concepts, but we are working through them together.

At some level, I am still allowed to suggest that he point the tire…

Benefits Beyond Spiritual

While your child's spiritual condition is the primary reason for engaging with them in the Word, there are many more benefits to this, not the least of which is academic. The Christian world view of an unchanging God who created and sustains the universe is at the root of the beginning of scientific inquiry. Theology is called the "Queen of the Sciences" because scientific method was developed from theological method. Many of the early scientists, Newton and Pascal to name two, were believers. Learning to analyze the scriptures equips your child with analytic tools that will serve them well in both literary and scientific pursuits.

If you recall, I mentioned that my college career was less than distinguished. I really did not know how to study. Working through the studies outlined in Chapter Four taught me how. I was accepted into seminary on academic probation due to my undergraduate performance. I graduated seminary with honors due in no small part to the way I had learned to study through my time in the scriptures. Developing a relationship with Christ through that study gave me an understanding of the importance of doing my best with what the Lord had given me.

This brings up the second benefit of engaging with your children in the Bible — discipline. I am not talking here about forced behavior or discipline in the sense of dealing with behavioral issues. Rather, I am referring to intrinsic motivation to do what one should be doing, the desire to be a good steward of one's gifts. It has been my experience that people who are engaged in the Bible in a consistent, deliberate way, who apply what they are learning to their lives, are more disciplined in their approach to life.

Reading skill is another benefit of doing consistent Bible study. The skills learned in doing analysis of scripture equip a person to think critically about what they may be reading. This helps a person become a lifelong learner, not only of scripture but of all literature.

Finally, and this should be painfully obvious, engaging with your children in the Word deepens and strengthens your relationship with them. That is a good thing.

You may be sitting there thinking that the opportunity to do this with your son or daughter has passed you by. No. Our God is a God of second, third, fourth, infinity chances. Grace. Engage. Do not demand, but engage in love. Start doing the study on your own, and share what you are learning. Pray. Ask the One who formed your son or daughter in the womb, personally, precisely, with passion, and for His purpose. Ask the One who loved them so much that He sacrificed His only Son on a Cross so that He could spend eternity with them. Ask Him who entrusted them to you. Ask to be able to meet with them to share the wonder of His majesty revealed through the written Word of God. Continue to ask. Continue to gently approach. The walls may begin to crumble and eventually fall.

In order to maximize this experience, there are some things you should avoid....

CHAPTER 6
What to Avoid

In order to be successful in this journey, you need to engage in the ways we have outlined. Success will come from the combination of your own spiritual walk along with consistent and meaningful interactions with your children. Much like other goals we set for ourselves, there are pitfalls to avoid. For instance, if you want to lose weight, you engage in exercise and watch what you eat. You avoid certain foods like ice cream, cake, donuts, you know, all the good stuff. But if you truly want to be successful in reaching your goal, you have to avoid these things. It is the same with leading your children in the Word.

One of the first things you have to avoid, in fact it should be a law, is:

Delegating the Development of Your Child

But this is a really easy trap to fall into for parents. There are such effective ministries out there - ministries I support - Young Life, AWANAS, Kanakuk, the church youth group. All of these are great resources, but they are not responsible for your children's foundation in the Word of God. You are. You have to be on top of what your children are learning. You have to view these ministries as a supplement to what you are already teaching your kids. It's not the other way around. When you sit down with God for your job review as a parent, I am not sure that He will respond well to you placing blame on the small group leader for your children's lack of spiritual maturity.

But there is a balance here. Don't you hate that word? We cannot help our kids become established in the Word by…

Being Demanding

Your children will not respond to this method, trust me. Or if they do, it will be all for external show and not be the truth in their hearts. We have all heard testimonies of people who have had "religion crammed down their throats." How do you respond to demands? If you are like me — not well.

In my opinion, Tom Landry was one of the best coaches — no — one of the best people that ever coached. He spoke once in Howard Hendricks' leadership class at Dallas Seminary while I was there. He shared about how at the beginning of each year he would meet with all of his players and ask them what their goals were for the year. He would then work with them individually to align their goals with the goals of the team so that if the goals of the team were met, their individual goals would be met. His genius with this was that he did not direct them or demand them to be on board with his goals, rather he helped them align with the team to get their goals met.

Jerry Ostroski is a member of our Sunday school class and is active in helping lead Men's Fraternity in our church. We meet together from time to time to coordinate Men's Fraternity. Jerry is large. At 6' 3" and 327 pounds, he played eight seasons with the

Buffalo Bills. He has recently been the strength coach at the University of Tulsa, his alma mater, and at the prep school Holland Hall. We were talking after Sunday school one day about the need to share the gospel and why people were not more involved in spiritual growth. He made the comment that working with people was a lot like coaching, you had to figure out their strengths and bring them out of their comfort zones so they could develop those strengths. He said that if people were not stretched, they would not grow.

There is a balance with these two perspectives that is really challenging. If we push our children too hard they will resist, and appropriately so. If we come alongside with encouragement and model what we are suggesting, we will help them grow most effectively.

If we make demands, they may comply externally, but they will not develop the internal motivation and personal relationship with Christ that will serve them when life gets hard.

Being Legalistic

This is closely related to being demanding. Requiring that your children perform week to week without regard for the ebbs and flows of life will communicate that the content of the study is more important than they are.

There have been numerous times in the past several years when John, Jeff, Brian, or I, because of circumstances like travel, job disruptions, major exams, client demand, and family issues, have not finished the study. We did not beat up the one who had the challenge. We still met and talked about what was going on in our lives. Sometimes we did read through or discuss part of what those of us who had finished the schedule had learned. But typically, we would just meet and talk and spend quality time together.

Now, I have tried it the other way. When Jenny and I were in collegiate ministry, I was not as flexible, understanding, nice, (not sure what the right word is here), and as a result, I am still looking for some of the people I interacted with back then to ask their forgiveness for pushing them so hard and driving them away.

The objective is not to just do the study. It is to develop a heart for God and His Word in the midst of dealing with life. The goal must be to communicate so your kids understand that this study is important and has great value, but to communicate that their value is not any less if they have not finished or performed to your satisfaction. That will only drive them away.

Becoming Proud

For years I carried a card in my wallet that I have since lost, and I cannot find the source of the quote. But it essentially said that one of the dangers of studying was that a person will study one subject deeply and it will consume their thoughts and focus. Because they have studied it and know it so well, they make it central to their understanding of the Christian life, looking down on those who do not understand or have not attempted to understand their perspective. Essentially, their commitment to this one portion of the faith overshadows all else. Grace, love, and compassion are all subordinated to this one idea. The person becomes arrogant and unapproachable.

And that is an accurate description of arrogance and pride. It also portrays the attitude of the people to whom Christ was talking in John 5. If you find that the Bible is making you proud, you are not applying it correctly. This is almost impossible to determine on your own; God will allow other people (even sometimes our own wives) to clue us in — if we let them.

As an example of humility, we can look at the progression of Paul's descriptions of himself throughout his ministry:

Galatians 2:6 — "But from those who were of high reputation (what they were makes no difference to me; God shows no partiality)—well, those who were of reputation contributed nothing to me."

1 Corinthians 15:9 — "For I am the least of the apostles, and not fit to be called an apostle, because I persecuted the church of God."

2 Corinthians 11:5 — "For I consider myself not in the least inferior to the most eminent apostles."

1 Timothy 1:15 — "It is a trustworthy statement, deserving full acceptance, that Christ Jesus came into the world to save sinners, among whom I am foremost of all."

The longer he walked with God the more humble he became. When we come face to face with God we are revealed as we are, unworthy to be in the room. It is by His grace that we stand and by His mercy that we have any influence at all.

As we study we become more and more familiar with the text and its contents. We will develop convictions about different aspects of the Christian experience. Some of those are not negotiable: namely salvation by faith in Christ alone, the deity of Christ, the resurrection, the authority of the Word of God, things to which the Bible speaks clearly and forcefully. However, there are other issues such as the method of baptism and spiritual gifts in which there seems to be some latitude. We need to hold our convictions in an open hand. We need to be willing to examine our positions under the light of scripture, understanding that we may not have fully understood some portion of His Word.

One of the reasons this is important is that we can learn from our children. They will have different gifts and experiences than we have. If we do not listen to them with an open heart and mind as they explore the scriptures, then we will shut down their curiosity and willingness to share. You have probably known people who are unapproachable in some area of knowledge. You may have been in a situation where you thought that they were mistaken or slightly off on a point. You know the feeling of being shut down and shut out.

I am not advocating acceptance of error. I am advocating the freedom to allow people the room they need to grow and develop and the ability to listen to others who see things differently in scripture than you do.

Which leads us to another parenting style that you may want to avoid with your children...

Preaching

It is really tempting when our kids ask a loaded question or a topic comes up in conversation that we feel we need to back up the truck and dump it.

"Daddy, where did I come from?" the seven-year-old asked. It was a moment for which her parents had carefully prepared. They took her into the living room, pulled out the encyclopedia and several other books, and explained all they thought she should know about sexual attraction, affection, love, and reproduction. Afterward, they both sat back and smiled contentedly.

"Does that answer your question?" her father asked.

"Not really," the little girl said. "Judy said she came from Detroit. I want to know where I came from."

Wow. It is crucial to understand the question. The best way to do that is to ask clarifying questions to determine what information is needed. It is better to ask questions and give a short follow-up assignment than to give a long monotonous answer. We all know those who when asked for the time will explain how to craft a watch. We avoid them. So will our kids.

There was a situation with Jeff one evening; I hesitate to share it because it is a controversial issue in the Church. You may not agree with where I stand in my understanding of this issue. That is OK. I do not share this in an attempt to sway your opinion, rather it is an example of using questions and dialogue rather than monologue to lead your children in their journey of developing their convictions and application of the Word of God.

I was in my study one evening when Jeff came in from his small group meeting. My study is the first room to the left of our front door. Jeff entered the room and sat down with a troubled look on his face.

I asked him what was bothering him. He told me that they had been studying 1 Timothy in his small group, and this week they were in chapter 2. In verse 12 they read, "But I do not allow a woman to teach or exercise authority over a man, but to remain quiet." He said that the leader of the study explained that this was a cultural issue and did not apply any longer.

I questioned him further, and he told me that he didn't feel that the leader was on target. He then asked for my opinion. In turn, I asked him what Paul was referring to in the passage of 1 Timothy. He answered correctly that it was the order of creation and the order of the fall. I suggested that he go back to Genesis and reread Genesis 1 – 3 since that is the passage to which Paul was referring. I told him specifically to read the chapters, consider them, and then return and we'd talk about it some more. He left the office to do just that.

About thirty minutes later he walked back into my office. I asked him what he had learned. He said that as he read through the passages and compared them to what Paul was saying in 1 Timothy, he did not see how they could be considered cultural and no longer applicable. This created an issue for him because we go to a church that places women in leadership over men in some areas. I asked him what he was going to do. He thought for a minute and decided that when the women who usually taught in the high school worship service stood up to teach, he would quietly excuse himself and go somewhere in the building and read his Bible. I told him that was a good plan.

The point here is not the conclusion he came to, but rather the way he got there. I could have told him my position; I did not. Instead, I asked him to look at the scripture more closely and to compare and contrast what was being said in the Bible with the position of the leader. He came up with what he thought to be accurate. Then he had to apply it in his situation. I could have suggested several different ways to deal with the dilemma. But I asked him what he thought he should do. He came up with a good solution based on his understanding of the text. I was pleased with his decision because it treated those that took a differing view with dignity.

There are a couple of underlying currents here that may be important. As I have shared this story with men, there has been some concern expressed that they would not have been able to refer their son to the correct passage. OK, that highlights what we have already mentioned in Chapter Two, which is that we have to be in the Word for ourselves. If we have not studied and thought an issue through, we will not be equipped to lead others as they are seeking answers to their questions. But we can always investigate the question with them. A good response may be, "I am not sure about that. Why don't we carve out some time and look at the Bible together on this?" That sets you up to do a topical study with your child.

Another important issue here is that we have to trust the Holy Spirit and the Word of God. When confronted with what I considered to be an error in someone's understanding of scripture, there were times when I would get a knot in my stomach and begin a fervent assault on their position. I felt that it was essential to the successful plan of God to correct what I saw to be an error. I am learning that what the Bible says about itself is true. It is living and active and sharper than any two-edged sword, piercing as to the division of soul and spirit. It is I who has to trust that if I share the Word of God with my kids, the Holy Spirit will use His sword; He will lead them into all truth.

It seems to me that this is part of the rest that Hebrews talks about. It is incumbent on me to get to know the Lord and scripture well;

then share that knowledge passionately with others, not just my children. What follows is out of my hands. I trust that God, who made the one I shared with and sent His son to die for them, will use His truth to draw them to Himself.

Using Aids

In our quest to understand more of God's Word, there are multiple aids available to us. There are commentaries, study Bibles, video series, devotionals, and audio series, all of which have great value. They can help us validate the conclusions we have formed from our studies.

Perhaps counterintuitively, I am going to suggest that you avoid using them or at least be very careful to not become dependent. This may seem to contradict the notion that you need to get to know scripture well, but it actually is for your benefit.

Commentaries

When used correctly, commentaries can be of great benefit in our study of scripture. One of the best books I have ever read is *How to Read a Book.* There is a section in the book about the use of commentaries; it is so beneficial, and I use it in all of my workshops.

How to Use Commentaries and Abstracts[1]

---

[1] Mortimer J. Adler. and Charles Van Doren, *How to Read a Book: The Classic Guide to Intelligent Reading* (New York: Simon and Schuster, 1972), 174-176. This is excerpted here. This book is mentioned in the annotated bibliography as perhaps the best book on how to learn.

A third category of extrinsic aids to reading includes commentaries and abstracts. The thing to emphasize here is that such works should be used wisely, which is to say sparingly. There are two reasons for this.

The first is that commentators are not always right in their comments on a book. Sometimes, of course, their works are enormously useful, but this is true less often than one could wish...

The second reason for using commentaries sparingly is that, even if they are right, they may not be exhaustive. That is, you may be able to discover important meanings in a book that the author of a commentary about it has not discovered. Reading a commentary, particularly one that seems very self-assured, thus tends to limit your understanding of a book, even if your understanding, as far as it goes, is correct.

Hence, there is one piece of advice that we want to give you about using commentaries. Indeed, this comes close to being a basic maxim of extrinsic reading. Whereas it is one of the rules of intrinsic reading that you should read an author's preface and introduction before reading his book, the rule in the case of extrinsic reading is that you should not read a commentary by someone else until after you have read the book. This applies particularly to scholarly and critical introductions. They are properly used only if you do your best to read the book first, and then and only then apply to them for answers to questions that still puzzle you. If you read them first they are likely to distort your reading of the book. You will tend to see only the points made by the scholar or critic and fail to see other points that may be just as important.

There is considerable pleasure associated with the reading of such introductions when it is done in this way. You have read the book and understood it. The writer of the introduction has also read it, perhaps many times, and has his own understanding of it. You approach him, therefore, on essentially equal terms. If you read his introduction before reading the book, however, you are at his mercy.

Heeding this rule, that commentaries should be read after you have read the book that they expound and not before, applies also to handbooks. Such works cannot hurt you if you have already read the book and know where the handbook is wrong, if it is. But if you depend wholly on the handbook, and never read the original book, you may be in bad trouble.

And there is this further point. If you get into the habit of depending on commentaries and handbooks, you will be totally lost if you cannot find one. You may be able to understand a particular book with the help of a commentary, but in general you will be a worse reader.

The rule of extrinsic reading given here applies also to abstracts and plot digests. They are useful in two connections, but in those two only. First, they can help to jog your memory of a book's contents, if you have already read it. Ideally, you made such an abstract yourself, in reading the book analytically, but if you have not done so, an abstract or digest can be an important aid. Second, abstracts are useful when you are engaged in syntopical reading,

> *and wish to know whether a certain work is likely to be germane to your project. An abstract can never replace the reading of a book, but it can sometimes tell you whether you want or need to read the book or not.*

I can't say it any better. Prof Hendricks has said on more than one occasion that we would be much better served reading the text than reading books about the text. The reason is that the text is inspired, living and active; words written about the text, although at times helpful, are not inspired, living and active. Studying the passage before you consult the commentary places you in dialogue with the author. That is the benefit. You approach not to hear what you should have gotten out of the text, but to compare and contrast.

Which leads us to the next thing to avoid...

Study Bibles

The same principle applies. Most of the study Bibles I have seen have a line somewhere on the page. The text of the book is above the line, and the comments on the verses are below the line. The text above the line is the inspired Word of God. The text below the line is not. Stay above the line. Or better yet, get a Bible that does not have a line at all.

There are at least two reasons for this. The first is outlined above. But the second may be more important. When we are struggling with a passage and the "answer" is there on the page, rather than think, pray, or consult other scripture, it is much easier to drop below the line to get the "answer." While this may satisfy our desire for "clarity," it robs us of the process of coming to our own understanding of the text. Perhaps more importantly, it robs us of time before God wrestling with the text and having the Holy Spirit lead us to deeper comprehension. It short-circuits that relationship.

The promise of God in John 16:13-14 is worth reviewing here, "But when He, the Spirit of truth, comes, He will guide you into all the truth; for He will not speak on His own initiative, but whatever He hears, He will speak; and He will disclose to you what is to come. He will glorify Me, for He will take of Mine and will disclose it to you." I urge you again lean first on the Holy Spirit and the text before you consult what is written below the line.

Focusing on Knowledge

We have covered this before, but it is critical so I will say it again. I learned it is OK to repeat myself from 2 Peter 1:13 and 3:1. The purpose of getting into the Word of God is not to make us smarter and to increase our knowledge, rather it is for us to get to know Christ. The focus of our studies should be to become better acquainted with our Lord.

During the workshops, I mention to the men that matching up the prophets with the corresponding Israelite kingdom is not the objective. Nor am I interested in being able to list the kings in order for either kingdom. While those things are helpful in that they can give us insight into how God has worked in the past, they are not paramount. Being able to beat our friends in Bible trivia, while satisfying, is not the objective. Knowing Christ is.

Living in a Hurry

We live in a fast-paced culture. We are used to and demand answers quickly. Google has spoiled us. Actually it is the Internet that has spoiled us. Across the major search engines, there are about 213 million searches a day that add up to 6.4 billion a month. That is more than one search per person on the planet, and not everybody has a computer. The search time is short, returning answers in a matter of seconds. I do not watch network news for a lot of reasons. One of the main reasons is that I can get three or four perspectives on a story much quicker on line. I do not have to wait for the story in which I am interested to come up during the newscast. I can get the information when I want it. That is amplified even more now that I have fast Internet service on my iPhone. I am hardly ever more than a couple of seconds away from updates.

That is a two-edged sword. While it is great to have that level of information, it creates baseline impatience in my search for knowledge. I am less willing to stay with something if I can't get the answer quickly. I want the answer, and I want it now. This phenomenon extends to entertainment as well. I want the problem solved in thirty minutes or at most an hour. If the resolution extends to the next episode, there is a groaning that takes place. There are exceptions to this, *24* leaps to mind. But the standard fare follows the pattern.

The Bible, and by extension the Lord, follows a different pattern. He rewards time invested. The benefit from the Word is proportional to the time invested in it. If I skim the surface, I will glean a surface knowledge. It is a relational model. It takes time and conversation. It takes being still and enjoying the presence of the Lord.

In his book, *Spirit of the Disciplines,*[2] Dallas Willard examines the life of Jesus and the life of Paul. He looks for patterns of spiritual formation that we can emulate. The driving thought is that if we are going to live the life of Christ, we might want to do what He did. He validates this by examining how Paul emulated the things Jesus did. It puts a tangible answer to the question: "What would Jesus do?"

One of Willard's more intriguing observations, and there are many, is that Jesus and Paul spent a great deal of time in solitude and silence. He points out that after the busy days that Christ spent in ministry, He would pull away from the crowds to be alone. This disengagement from the demands on His time is a great model for us to follow. It is necessary; in order to get the time we need in the Word with the Lord, we must remove ourselves from the hectic pace. We have to unplug from the matrix. Turn off the cell phone. Get away from E-mail and the Internet. Be quiet. Be still. Take time.

Become Critical

This may seem redundant after the already mentioned notion of becoming proud. Criticism is different. As you become more and more familiar with the Bible, your confidence and convictions

---

[2] Dallas Willard, *The Spirit of the Disciplines: Understanding How God Changes Lives* (San Francisco: HarperSanFrancisco, 1988), the complete list is on page 158. To say that I highly recommend this book is a great understatement.

will deepen. You may find yourself in the company or in an audience of one who may not have the apparent depth of knowledge that you have attained. You may find yourself becoming critical of how they are handling their topic or the Word of God in general. It is not the case that you should accept uncritically all that you hear in a group setting. It is the case that you should approach those with whom you do not find alignment with grace and compassion.

I have failed in this area many times, so I know that it is not effective. One of the verses that keeps coming up in my life is Proverbs 15:2: "The tongue of the wise makes knowledge acceptable, But the mouth of fools spouts folly." That verse tells me that I can turn truth into folly by the way that I say it.

The president of a denominational seminary spoke to our Sunday school class once. He gave an excellent presentation on 1 Samuel; excellent that is until he got to application. He then proceeded to commit theological malpractice in front of close to 75 people. What do I mean by theological malpractice? He took the Bible out of their hands. Up to the point of his application, we could follow all that he was saying and track his points through scripture. But when began the application, he used a series of logical fallacies to make a point that was unsupported by the text from which he was speaking and built the case for this point on an obscure scholar of which he alone had knowledge. So essentially he was saying to the class, you cannot hope to understand this because you do not have my knowledge and position.

My passion is to guide people into the Word of God, to help equip them to study and meet with God on their own. This leader was communicating through his teaching, demeanor, and example, that the group could not understand scripture without his help. Men have died to put the Word of God in our hands, how dare he attempt to remove it! In case you missed it, he made me mad. I was critical of his approach.

As he finished, I raised my hand. At that point my wife, who knows me very well, wanted to be anywhere but in that classroom.

I said, "I am not sure what grade you would have received on that presentation at your seminary, but where I attended you would have gotten an F."

That was not the most helpful, attractive, or winsome thing I could have said. I let my emotions overrun my judgment. I was right to question, but I could have done it less confrontationally in a way that invited dialogue rather than shut it down. You may think I should have just kept my mouth shut. Well, that would have been a better idea than what I did. However, when one is damaging people by what he is saying, as this man was, he has to be confronted. I just did not do it properly. I later wrote a five-page response to his lesson enumerating specifically the errors he made in application. I did not send it to him; it would have made no difference.

Becoming Intolerant

You may have encountered people who have become entrenched in their positions. Prof[3] said people like this were suffering from "hardening of the categories." I teach — well that is a bit of a stretch — it is more like herding cats at a men's Bible study at

---

[3] Howard Hendricks – Professor at Dallas Theological Seminary

0630 on Tuesday mornings at our church. One morning a couple of men came to the study who participated well throughout the lesson. Toward the end of our time, they tried to take over the discussion and move into an area that could only be described as Gnostic. That is, it was a view of scripture that required one to look for hidden codes and meanings. These men had invested a lot of time and effort into this errant view of scripture. But we were able to keep the discussion on track.

Later, I had opportunity to speak with these men individually about their approach to scripture, but they were not in the least open to discussion. They had "higher" knowledge and did not need others to agree or disagree. They would not participate in a conversation about their opinions. They did not return to the study, though they were invited and welcome. Since we did not buy into their direction, they did not want to participate.

Proverbs 18:1–2 says, "He who separates himself seeks his own desire, He quarrels against all sound wisdom. A fool does not delight in understanding, But only in revealing his own mind." It is dangerous to study in a vacuum. We all need others who will check our thinking and our approach to scripture. We can never allow ourselves to get to the place where we are not open to discussion. That is dangerous to an extreme. We need to be with people who will encourage us and speak into our lives when we are in error. Otherwise, as Proverbs says, we are fools.

So while it is important to develop our walk with God through the scripture and involve our children in the process, it is also important that we avoid the behaviors outlined here. They will either hinder our growth, drive our children away from us, or both.

I have worked for a long time as a consultant in business operations and focused on developing and implementing processes to help businesses be more effective in what they do. All processes, no matter how well thought out and implemented will have exceptions. Special circumstances that render the normal process useless or else impossible to implement without significant modification. Next we will look at some special circumstances that will challenge both your walk with God and leading your children.

CHAPTER 7
Special Circumstances

The reality is: we live in a broken world. In the Church and in the community, our world contains broken people and broken families. If you are in this situation or if you are in a blended family, you have issues to deal with that I have never experienced — only observed. What should you do? How does one approach the task of engaging kids in the Word in this situation? What are some of the pitfalls?

Or you have prayed and wanted children for your entire life. Your child is born after nine months of anticipation, but then you are told that there is an issue. Your life is changed forever. Your child has Down's syndrome, cerebral palsy, autism, or some other challenge. Now all of the things you were planning or looking forward to have been replaced by visits to doctors and research on your child's situation. You may be numb.

That is reality. How do we deal with it effectively?

Divorce

Divorce in our culture is near epidemic. Statistics vary, but close to one in three marriages end in divorce according to a March,

2008 study by the Barna Group.[1] Trouble is, that number does not change much if one is a born-again evangelical Christian. That fact begs a number of questions that are outside the scope of this book.[2] But it does tell me that one in three people who are holding this book have experienced a divorce.

Mothers

One of the hardest challenges for a divorced mother is how to raise a son. After all, a woman cannot teach a boy how to be a man; she is not one. So what is she to do? I was faced with this when I received an E-mail from a lady in our church who wanted to know if I had anything to help with her son. I was not prepared at the time. I am ashamed to say that I did not have an adequate answer for her. The answer is developing as I learn from other ministries.

---

[1] The Barna Group, Ltd., "New Marriage and Divorce Statistics Released," (March 31, 2008), http://www.barna.org/barna-update/article/15-familykids/42-new-marriage-and-divorce-statistics-released (Accessed February 17, 2010).

[2] Divorce has become culturally accepted, in large part because of an incorrect view of marriage. While neither the issue of divorce nor its impact on children is the focus of this book, I felt it was too prevalent to ignore. The research uncovering the negative consequences of divorce on children is massive. Especially of interest is the impact of fatherless homes. The research is staggering in both volume and findings. Equally staggering is the cultural commitment to ignore the devastating impact of divorce and fatherless families on children, in order to deny and cover up the research. Spend a few minutes on these websites: www.fathers.com; www.fatherhood.org; www.fathersforlife.org. Skim the research sections, and you will begin to get a feel for the magnitude of the challenge, or Google "effects of divorce on children."

Get Men's Group at Church Involved

Young men need male mentors. That should be one of the focuses of the men's ministry at any church. If your church's men's ministry does not engage with young men who are in need of a man in their life, talk to the leader or the pastor to see if you can get them on board. In lieu of that, ask your pastor for recommendations of men who can be a mentor for your son. Getting your son connected with a mentor will not completely nullify the effects of growing up without a resident father, but it will help immensely.

If you are reading this and you are involved in men's ministry at your church, make sure this issue is addressed for mothers in this dilemma. It is our responsibility as men to lead in this area. James 1:27 tells us that, "Pure and undefiled religion in the sight of our God and Father is this: to visit orphans and widows in their distress, and to keep oneself unstained by the world." It could be argued that a child that has been abandoned by his father fits that category. He is certainly in distress. He certainly needs to have men in his life who can not only be a model of a godly man, but also who can roughhouse with him, take him to games, and show him how to study the Word. If the divorcee has a daughter, she also will need a male authority figure in her life who will be a stabilizing influence.

When the father leaves the family, many children feel that they are somehow at fault. The child aches for his father's influence and at some level wonders if men are reliable. All children need godly role models in their lives. The impact of that ministry in their lives would be difficult to exaggerate.

Fathers

If you are a divorced, non-custodial father, your responsibilities have not ended with the divorce becoming final; they have just gotten more complex. You are still Dad, regardless of where you live. You are still accountable for your child's spiritual development, not to the church, but to God.

First Timothy 5:8 tells us that, does it not? "But if anyone does not provide for his own, and especially for those of his household, he has denied the faith and is worse than an unbeliever." As a divorced father, you cannot leave the development of your children to your wife alone. You have to engage. Obviously there are challenges associated with this. Your wife may not want you around; you may want to avoid being around her. One or the other of you may have an opportunity or demand to move to a different city. There can be a myriad of other challenges. Nevertheless, you are still accountable for the spiritual development of your children. I am not trying to be harsh here; the reality is, this is a tough situation. You will have to be tough to face it and be successful in fighting for your kids. So what should you do?

Prayer

If you are not engaged in prayer about this responsibility, start now. Pray for your wife. Pray for your relationship with her. Why? One of the realities that has been revealed by the research is that if the relationship between the husband and wife continues to be tumultuous after the divorce, the impact on the children is greater.[3] So pray for the relationship to improve. Pray for your

---

[3] Brian D'Onofrio, "Divorce, Dad, and the Well-Being of Children: Answering Common Research Questions," page 3, Institute for American Values, Center for marriage and Families, Research Brief No. 12, July 2008 (PDF document). http://www.fatherhood.org/research.asp (accessed February 20, 2010).

children defensively. Pray against feelings of abandonment and insecurity. Pray for openness to your sharing the Word with them, and pray for time with them in the Word.

Counsel of the Pastor

Talk to your pastor. Tell him what is going on in the relationship with your children and your wife. Tell him about your struggles and what you want to do about them. Let him be a sounding board for you. Listen to what he tells you. Pray with him over your wife and children.

Group of Men – Band of Brothers

You need a support group. You need men who will pray with you for your wife and kids. You need men who will stand with you against the enemy when he is seeking to devour the hearts of your children. You need men with whom you can process the time you spend with your children and give you counsel on what you should be sharing with them. You need brothers who will shoot straight with you and not put up with your bad attitudes, who will support you, and pray for and with you as you continue to fight for your kids' hearts. You need them for all three of the situations considered in this chapter. Frankly, you need them whether you are in any of these situations or not.

Examine Your Heart

Motives are tricky things. Honestly examine your heart. Why do you want to engage with your children? Talk this over with your band of brothers and your pastor. If you are doing this to somehow compete with or hurt your wife, that is a challenge. You still need to engage, but you also need to get your heart right. This is not about you. This is not about trying to be more important than your wife; it is about what your kids need from you to be healthy. It is about them and your responsibility to them as a dad.

Invite

As we said in Chapter Five, do not force this on your kids. You invite them to join you. This is especially important in this situation. They may be angry with you, and they may not want to do this. You may be in a situation where your visits with them are characterized by conflict so you must win their trust.

If they resist joining you on this journey, do not demand. Pray. Pray for a breakthrough in the relationship. It may take time to gain their trust, and they may want to see if you are really going to continue in the Word. To start share small bites of what you are learning from the Word with them in passing.

Commit Not to Miss

Do not cancel on them. OK, life happens, so if you get sick or have to go out of town on business, reschedule. But you have to be consistent. Your kids are hurt; they are insecure in their relationship with you and with themselves. At some level they are not sure that you love them. You have to work hard to regain their trust. If you allow a pattern of missing your time with them to develop, you will do damage.

Make Hard Decisions

This brings me to a really tough concept. You may have to change your goals in business and life to go after your kids. If your career requires you to be on the road for long periods of time, you may have to change careers in order to make time to see them. You have to decide what is more important.

A key leader in our church suffered through a divorce. It was not his choice; his wife filed. I do not know the details, but I know how he responded. When his wife moved to another town in another state, taking the kids, he moved to that town and changed careers in order to continue to be in their lives. That was tough. That was placing them and their needs before his. That is what we are exhorted to do in Philippians 2, is it not? "Do nothing from selfishness or empty conceit, but with humility of mind regard one another as more important than yourselves; do not merely look out for your own personal interests, but also for the interests of others."

That is much easier to read and write than it is to live. It is not only required from those of us who have to deal with our kids in a divorce situation, but it is also required from all of us who are apprentices of Jesus Christ. In fact, regardless of our marital situation, we are to put our wives and children's interests ahead of ours. We have no chance of doing this in our own strength. Should we try, and I have, we will frequently become bitter, resentful, and angry.

The only way to pull this off is to do what we learned in the verse analysis study in Chapter Two. John 15:5 says, "abide in Christ." Through the power of the Holy Spirit, we have to remain in Christ. Which means that if we are serious about putting others' interests, including those of our children, ahead of ours — if we really want to see them walk with God — we have to abide first. That is the essence of leadership, is it not? We have to do first what we are leading others to do. It will be a battle. It will be resisted. We will cover that in more detail in the next chapter. This essentially means that we need to spend time with Christ in the Word and prayer. Not just doing the tasks and going through the motions, rather taking the time to really soak in the Word and have it transform our lives. That cannot be short-circuited. There is no short cut. We just have to do it.

Prepare for the Hard Questions

If you are successful in engaging your children with you on this journey, at some point the Word of God is going to reveal that you and/or your wife may have made a choice that does not align with scripture. Specifically, when you come to the passages on divorce, you may face some hard questions from your kids. You may feel that you do not want to start down that path because you do not want to have to deal with the issues that led to the divorce. I can understand that. But you see, this is true for all of us that come to the Word with our children. We will have to face the mirror of the Word of God and see our sinfulness revealed in front of our children regardless of whether we are divorced.

There are at least three things we can choose to do when the hard questions are raised.

One potentially destructive response is to avoid the question. For example, you answer with, "You would not understand," or "We will talk about that when you are older'" or some other deflecting response. In some cases there may be legitimate reasons for delaying the conversation. You should talk this through with your pastor or counselor who knows the details of the situation.

Get their take on whether you should delay talking about this with your child when it arises. I would suggest you have that conversation with the pastor or counselor prior to engaging with your child.

Most of the time when I want to deflect a question, it is because I am not secure with the answer I have, or I am ashamed of what the answer will reveal about me. In most cases, the first reason is not legitimate. The second isn't either.

When asked pointed questions by our kids, we need to respond to them with integrity. They will know if we're not being honest, and it will erode their trust in us. I was talking to Joe Scruggs about this (Joe is the pastor of our church and a clinical psychologist.) He pointed out that children can also lose confidence in themselves. They perceive that there is a problem in the family, but when they ask about it are told that everything is all right or their question is deflected. It can cause them to question their ability to perceive reality. The inner conversation goes something like, "No one is acknowledging what I am seeing here. I must not be able to tell what is really going on."

When John was a sophomore in college, he worked for me in the summer doing desktop support in our IT department. One evening as he came into my home office, I was working on a project that was taking an inordinate amount of time due to some bugs that were in the software we were using. He sat down, and in tears, asked me why I was working so much. He said that he had come to work with my company so he could get more time with me. But he observed correctly that I had been doing nothing but work since he had been home. He pointed out that I had even worked through our "vacation." He was right. I needed to get my eyes off of the project and on to the family. I had gotten my priorities all balled up. It took my twenty-year-old son to correct me. It was not the last time.

The second way we deal with hard questions is to blame someone else. This can be an almost irresistible force when there are other people involved in the issue, especially in the case of divorce. It might be easy to say, "It's your mom's fault." And in truth, it would be consistent with the way men have been dealing with getting caught in sin since the garden.

> [11]And He said, "Who told you that you were naked? Have you eaten from the tree of which I commanded you not to eat?" [12]*The man said, "The woman whom You gave to be with me, she gave me from the tree, and I ate."*[4]

IT WAS NOT MY FAULT! How many times in our lives have we said that? In fact, it probably was at least partially our fault. But, as you see, we came by that tendency genetically. Our father Adam handled getting caught with his hand in the cookie jar — umm — tree of knowledge, by blaming his wife, foreshadowing men's behavior throughout recorded history.

It is cowardly.

It communicates a lack of integrity.

It erodes trust.

It will eat away at you.

It is much better to respond with the third option. Admit your failure. This is hard. It requires us to admit weakness to those

---

[4] Genesis 3:11–12

whom we are supposed to be leading. We may think that it will cause them to think less of us. But the reality is, it will increase our credibility. When confronted by your child, you do not have to give details, all you have to do is admit to the fact that you made mistakes and/or poor choices.

The great thing about this approach, in addition to the fact that it allows you to talk about the forgiveness and grace of God, is it allows you to explore the way God uses broken people with your child. Even when we blow it — when we betray people the way Peter betrayed Christ, when we become angry and shun people like Paul did John Mark, when we steal and run away like Onesimus did to Philemon — God can still use us. This is not to condone sin, rather to highlight the grace of God to your child. Paul gives us a good perspective on this:

> *What shall we say then? Are we to continue in sin so that grace may increase? May it never be! How shall we who died to sin still live in it? Or do you not know that all of us who have been baptized into Christ Jesus have been baptized into His death? Therefore we have been buried with Him through baptism into death, so that as Christ was raised from the dead through the glory of the Father, so we too might walk in newness of life. For if we have become united with Him in the likeness of His death, certainly we shall also be in the likeness of His resurrection, knowing this, that our old self was crucified with Him, in order that our body of sin might be done away with, so that we would no longer be slaves to sin; for he who has died is freed from sin.*[5]

[5] Romans 12:1-7

Another advantage of admitting your failure to your children is that it creates an atmosphere where they can share struggles they are having with you. It opens up a deeper level of communication as you both engage in trusting the grace of God.

Engage for the Long Term

What we are talking about here is not a dip in, dip out type of exercise. This is a long-term commitment for all of us, through all phases of life. It's true for all who read this book; yet at some level, it is more important if you are dealing with children who are products of divorce. This is because children who have experienced divorce have challenges stemming from the divorce well into middle adulthood.[6] This underscores the need for a solid foundation in the Word of God for the child. It also suggests that you will need to continue to engage with them as long as you can. At some point, the touches may have to be done remotely. With the development of webcams and free webcam software, distance and co-location is less of a problem today than it has been.

To conclude, it is a long-term commitment for us to build into the lives of our children, whether we have experienced a divorce or not. If there is a divorce to deal with, it adds complexities that will make the task that much more difficult. All of us have to rely on the Spirit of God to engage successfully with our kids. We are not more or less dependent on Him due to our circumstances, there are just more circumstances with which to deal.

---

[6] D'Onofrio, page 2.

Blended Family

As divorce has increased, so have the instances of remarriage and the creation of blended families. Blended families have complexities that are increased as the number and sources of the children increase. As a father, you may be the father of some of the children in your family, the father of children of which you do not have custody, and the step-father of children of which you do have custody. We will consider your relationship with step-children here.

First, all of what we considered above applies here. If your child's biological parent is involved with them that may or may not make the task easier. There are a lot of variables. A few that come to mind:

1. The biological parent is a believer and wants to be involved with their children as we have described above.

2. The biological parent is a believer, but is not involved in the lives of his kids.

3. The biological parent is not a believer and wants to be involved with his kids. Their lifestyle and behavior is not a negative influence on the children.

4. Same as above, but the parent's lifestyle and behavior is a problem. They are not trying to undermine you.

5. Same as above, but the parent is trying to undermine you.

There are probably many other scenarios I have not considered.

These are complex enough. Number one is the best possible scenario. In this situation you are essentially on the same team, and you are reinforcing one other. The only thing here that you may need to watch out for is overwhelming and confusing the child on who is the ultimate authority. In this situation, it may be good to talk to the parent and strategize how to best work together to build up the child.

Murphy's Law suggests that this will not be the hand you are dealt. You may have to deal with #3 – #5. In that case you will obviously be in battle for the heart and mind of the child. This will be a spiritual battle that will not be won with logic.

For the past several months, I have been walking through situation #5 with a friend. They shared openly about the struggles occurring, and we have talked and prayed together over the situation. My friend has prayed, shared scripture and done all that either of us knows to do. There are two children involved. One has responded. One has not. It is a really tough fight. I share that because there are no guarantees, not for any of us. We pray and do our best in the counsel of the Lord, but we have to trust God for the results — a result which we may not ever see. It may take years for a child to respond. During that time they will be watching. They will be looking to see if what you say is real. Are you sticking with this Christ thing? Is it real to you? Will you finish well? It may be only then that they respond. You have to stay the course with your walk with God regardless of your child's response.

Be Available

Other than making sure you are walking with God personally and consistently, the best thing you can do is to be available for your children. Engaged, and not demanding but inviting. Let them know that you are always interested in sharing with them what you are learning. Be involved in their lives so you can speak appropriately from scripture as they encounter different issues. Deuteronomy 6:6-7 was never more powerful than in this situation. We have reviewed them before, but it bears repeating here: "These words, which I am commanding you today, shall be on your heart. You shall teach them diligently to your sons and shall talk of them when you sit in your house and when you walk by the way and when you lie down and when you rise up." Look for opportunities to share what you are learning from the Lord as you live life together.

Not preaching. Sharing. Not opening the Bible and showing them the passage, rather sharing it from your heart and life. You have to earn the right and the trust of the child before you can share more directly from the Word. I am referring at this point to older children. If you have been around them since they were young, you will have more freedom to share with them as we have described in Chapter Five.

Pray

I know I sound like a broken record here, but the reality is that bathing this situation in prayer is just about — no check that — is the most important thing you can do. These situations can be doubly tough. Second Corinthians 12:9 comes to mind, "And He has said to me, "My grace is sufficient for you, for power is perfected in weakness. Most gladly, therefore, I will rather boast about my weaknesses, so that the power of Christ may dwell in me." In scenarios like these, really in all of life, we have to embrace the fact that we are in need of God's grace and beseech Him to intervene on our behalf.

Special Needs

My brother-in-law has Down syndrome, and he is now 42 years old. In the past few years he has become increasingly non-verbal. We learned several years ago that individuals with Down syndrome begin to exhibit symptoms of Alzheimer's when they get older, and he seems to be following that path. He has been in a near constant conversation with a person he alone can see for the past fifteen years. He lives at home with his mom and dad who are now in their eighties.

When my brother-in-law was younger, he competed in the International Special Olympics. He learned to play the piano, drums, and flute. He played the flute before the church, so it has been difficult watching him withdraw.

My wife is a special education teacher with a master's degree in learning disabilities and works with children in a pre-kindergarten and kindergarten program. Most of her students are autistic. Each summer for the past ten years, we have traveled to Jenny's parent's home and brought her brother back to our house for four to six weeks.

I share that to give you some context.

Life Commitment

When you discover that the Lord has entrusted you with a child with special needs, your life changes. Your plans, dreams, schedule, retirement, social interactions, needs and hopes are irrevocably altered. Permanently. This is not an assignment from which one can resign. Of course this is true for all of us who have children. We are always and forever fathers. But, the demands on those of us who have children with special needs do not abate. My expectation for my four children is that at some point they will leave our nest and create their own. Get off the payroll. Get a job. Possibly get married and have a family. That is not the case with most children who are born with special needs. My in laws are in their eighties and still involved in daily caring for their son. It is a life commitment.

One of my neighbors has a son with Down syndrome, and his son is currently living in a group home. We ran into each other at Sam's Club the other day. He was explaining that his son, like Jenny's brother, is beginning to evidence symptoms of Alzheimer's. While our neighbor is not involved at this point in the daily care of his son, he is still financially responsible, and his son is never far from his mind.

How does one, as a father of a child with special-needs build into the child's life? Is it even reasonable? What if the child are profoundly challenged and non-responsive? What do we do?

Pray

You may be seeing a pattern here. In all situations we have to start with ourselves. If we are not walking with God — in His Word daily, and in communion with Him in prayer — it is impossible to handle well the challenges that come our way. This is true in the best of circumstances; it is certainly true when we are challenged with a child who needs extra attention and care.

We are always dependent on God. In the Psalms, we have a model for prayer when things seem to be crashing around us. I would recommend, if you have not already done so, that you take a month and read through the Psalms. There are 150 of them. It is an interesting exercise. If you take the day of the month, say the 22nd, read that psalm – 22. Then add 30, landing on 52; add 30 again, which is 82; then 112, and finally 142. You will read through all of them in a month. The challenge is Psalm 119 on which you may want to spend an entire day. As you read through, notice the attitude of the psalmists as they struggle with various issues of life. Some of them have subheadings to tell you what is going on at the time. You may notice a pattern. In a lot of cases the psalmist will begin by crying and complaining bitterly to God. About halfway through the psalm, the cry turns to praise. This pattern is evident especially in David's psalms; most of them are in 1-40.

David was, at times, confused, angry, and bitter, and he let God know about it. But God already knew. David poured his heart out, holding nothing back, resulting in an honesty in his dealings with God that led Luke to say of David in Acts 13:22 (quoting 1 Samuel 13:14) "he was a man after God's heart."

When we are in pain, like David, we need to tell God. When we are struggling, we need to tell Him. It is only as we walk closely with Him that we will be able to deal effectively with the realities He has given us to face.

The not so well hidden message throughout this book is that if we are going to help our children and deal well with the issues that are facing us and them, we have to be in the Word and in communion with God regularly through prayer.

So having that foundation, what can one do practically to lead a child with special needs?

Read

Read to them from the Word or from Bible story books. You may not get a response, but read anyway. It gives you time that is structured with them. It gives them your presence; they hear your voice. As we will talk about a little later, you do not know what they will hear and retain. If they can read, take turns reading together. If their attention span is short keep it short, and at their reading level. I mentioned the *Read Aloud Bible Stories* series in Chapter Five. When my brother-in-law is visiting, we will sometimes read those books with him. One of us will read a page, and then he will read the next. We alternate until we have finished the story.

Expose

Expose your child to as many experiences that incorporate the Word of God as possible. We have mentioned some of them in Chapter Five. Veggie Tales, McGee and Me, some of the Fox Faith movies, music, whatever you can find that has a Christian message. Have them interact with other children in Christian environments, Sunday school, and AWANAS. You may have to go with them.

You need other people who are believers engaged with your child.

Support

You need support. Find other believers going through the same challenges as you. Talk to your pastor about who may be in the area who can be of help. There are national organizations that give support to believers who have children with special needs. A quick Internet search turns up many options. I will not recommend any here because I have not thoroughly researched them. I have looked at their statements of faith as a starting place but cannot vouch for the way that they apply the scriptures.

I do not have all the answers. I am not sure that I even know all the right questions. I do know that our Father does. If you ask Him for help, He will give it to you.

My Brother-in-Law

I mentioned that my brother-in-law has Down syndrome. The thoughts I have shared here are based on the last thirty-two years of observing him and processing what I have seen with and through my wife's experience as a teacher of children with special needs.

Let me give you some examples.

Neil Sedaka

One evening I was in the back of my in-law's house. The room was originally my brother-in-law's, but had been transformed into a sort of entertainment center/spare bedroom. There was a rack of old 45 rpm records on a shelf. He was sitting next to me as I was going through them. At about the middle of the stack, there was a record with a blue label. When he saw it he became really excited. He said, "Laughter in the Rain," and asked for the record. He could not read the label from where he was sitting. He just knew it by sight. It was his favorite.

Jim Falk

Jim and Sandee Falk are some of our closest friends. We lived across the hall from each other at Michigan State and across town from each other in Knoxville while we were at the University of Tennessee. We ministered together at both schools.

When I graduated from Dallas Seminary, Jim came to the ceremony. He met my brother-in-law there for the first time, and they played a couple of card games together and talked. That was nineteen years ago. Nearly every time we have been on the phone with my brother-in-law for the past nineteen years, he has asked how Jim Falk is doing.

Bands, Movies, and Dogs

He was really into high school marching bands and had tapes of performances which he would watch over and over. He went to some of the contests locally and would play recordings of those bands again and again. He became fixated on some movies: "Jaws" was one that he really enjoyed, which led to looking at picture books about sharks for years. For a long while, Doberman Pinchers were another interest. He does not like real dogs at all, they scare him, but he loved their pictures and plastic replicas.

It has been interesting over the years to see that to which he has gravitated. There seemed to be some randomness to the objects of affection that he chose. But for the subjects on which he chose to focus, he retained interest and retains it still.

Expose your child to as much Christian experience as you can. Encourage the areas where they seem to have strong preference. Find media, toys, or examples of those things that have a biblical message. Trust God to implant this in their heart.

I realize that this is a long, hard road. I have watched in awe as my in-laws have cared for my brother-in-law. They increasingly have to do more and more for him to take care of his personal needs. When he was born, the doctors told my father-in-law to put his new son in an institution, but he and his wife vowed that it would never happen. It was a hard decision. It was firm. It has been costly. I honor them for sticking with it when it would have been so easy to give up.

If the Lord chooses to give you one of these children, it will be challenging. It will be good.

In these three situations, there are no clean, easy, fail-safe answers. In fact, there are no clean, easy, fail-safe answers for any of us. Life is messy. It is a broken world. We are broken people. We simply have to keep pressing on through the power of the Holy Spirit.

CHAPTER 8

Resistance to Implementation

By now we have laid a solid foundation — that we as fathers have a primary responsibility to build spiritually into our children's lives. If you have made it this far into our discussion, I assume that you want to engage in that responsibility in a meaningful way.

So what could possibly keep you from being successful? You will probably face some strong resistance.

There are at least three sources of this resistance:

- Your own inertia
- Your children's inertia or attitude
- Your sworn enemy's commitment

Your Inertia

If it is the case that you have not been doing regular Bible study up to this point, you have to start. That may seem obvious, but as you know starting anything new requires change. Most of us do not accomplish change well. To add something to your schedule, you have to change it. Perhaps you will have to eliminate some things you are currently doing, perhaps some good things.

I have to exercise. For years it was something I did to maintain health and fitness. I ran until I lost my knees; I swam until it became too burdensome to find a place to swim; I started riding a road bike, and now exercise is essential. Two years ago this July, I woke up on a Sunday morning in excruciating pain. A disk in my back had herniated. After a morning in the ER, I was given a set of exercises to see if I could avoid surgery, and I was told to stay off of my road bike. So for the next several months, for about one and a half to two hours a day, I did exercises to strengthen my core to try to avert the surgery. So far it has worked. But it is hard to make that time to exercise, especially when the best time for me is early in the morning which coincides with the best time to meet with men over the Word. Something had to change. Last summer, I was able to get back on a bike. I obtained a recumbent that does not strain my back. But to ride it consistently requires time.

The reality is that we do what is important to us. As adults we learn what we want to learn or feel that we have to know to survive. I play guitar and have for nearly 50 years. I am pretty good. I cannot count the number of people who have come up to me after hearing me play to say, "I have always wanted to learn to play guitar." When I was younger and not so wise, I would typically respond, "No you haven't. If you really wanted to learn how to play guitar, you would have." While I am nicer than that now, it is still true. We make time for and do things that are important to us.

My grandmother loved *As the World Turns*. Back in the early '60s, she was living with us. I was in my early teens, and it was before VCRs or DVRs. Whenever we were out shopping at the time when the show would air, my assignment was to find a TV and watch it to tell her what happened. Today, people will not answer phones while *24, American Idol, Survivor* or whatever is on. They plan their schedules around those shows.

I am not against TV. I love *24*. But my priority is time in the Word. I have found that I cannot regularly watch TV and get the time in the Word that I require. So I choose to limit my TV to one or two shows a week. You will have to make similar changes. As I mentioned earlier in the book, we all are equal in one sense. We all have one hundred and sixty-eight hours a week. It does not matter if you are Bill Gates, the President of the United States, or a janitor — you have one hundred and sixty-eight hours. It is your choice how you use that time.

So if you are going to add the discipline of regular Bible study to an already hectic schedule, and on top of that a time to meet with your son or daughter on that study, you will have to make some changes. You may have to alter your work schedule. You may have to alter your goals. In extreme cases you may have to change your job or turn down an opportunity.

We all remember where we were on the morning of September 11th, 2001. I was consulting at a company at the time. That gig ended quickly. If you were in business then, you remember the climate. No one knew what would happen so people did not take risks and did not, for the most part, spend money. I found myself working two jobs; mortgage banker by day and a night manager of a Quik Trip convenience store overnight. I slept from about 4 p.m. to 11 p.m. most days. During this time I was leading a Bible study at our church on Wednesday morning. Quik Trip is a really great company. They have been written up in the *Harvard Business Review* and are in the Top 40 of the best places to work on the Forbes list. About six months after I started working there, I was asked to move to another store. At Quik Trip that is the way to advance. You move continually to higher volume stores and then up in responsibility. My reason for working there was that the only way into the corporate office was through the stores. I was excited about the move until I found that I would no longer have Tuesdays off, which meant that I could not lead the Wednesday morning study. I turned the move down. My priority was that study.

You may think I was irresponsible. "You should have provided for your family," you may say. True. However, it is also true that Jesus tells us in Matthew 6:33: "But seek first His kingdom and His righteousness, and all these things will be added to you." He wants us to trust Him. He wants us to put Him and our walk with Him first, and trust Him to provide. We did not miss a meal. Throughout all of these years, we have made every house and car payment and gotten four kids through college. He asked us to trust Him. We did. He provided. You may have to exercise a new level of trust to overcome inertia to get started in this process.

Your Children's Inertia

The second area of resistance you may encounter is that your kids may not want to engage. If your kids are younger, this is easier to overcome. If they are older, there are different challenges.

Let's start with the older kids. As we grow and develop as people, we assemble a set of maxims and behaviors that help us to cope with how we think the world works. That is our world view. Part of the challenge of the Christian life is to determine how our world view differs from the reality of what God is doing and transform our world view to align with His. Typically, our kids will initially embrace our world view. They are looking to us for explanations about what is happening around them. As children grow older, they begin to form their own world view. Their experiences will play a large part in their developing world view. It will diverge from yours at some level, and in some cases radically. That is part of the separation that takes place as they grow up. Part of your older children's world view is how they see and relate to you, from their perspective, effectively. If you have not been engaged consistently in dialogue about spiritual issues as they have grown, or they have not seen you engaged in spiritual growth or Bible study, your invitation may be difficult for them to process. Add that to the busyness issue that all of us have to deal with, and the challenge is compounded.

So, how do we proceed? Understanding that your older child may be taken a bit off guard by your suggestion that you study the Bible together is more than half of the battle, or if not, some significant percentage thereof. So after you have acknowledged that and accepted it, you should pray. If God can move the hearts of kings like channels of water (Proverbs 21:1), he can probably do the same with your child. You may want to enlist a team of men to pray with you about this. I would suggest this strongly. If they know your son or daughter, they may be able to suggest ways in which to best present the idea.

Now invite. The key word here is invite. It is not a command or even a strong recommendation. If you have not had a habit of study in the past, you may want to say something like, "Son, I am going to be working on applying some things I have learned about studying the Bible. I am not an expert on this. I still have a lot of questions, but I would like to work through this with you.

I would value your perspective on this process and what the Bible says. I thought we could meet together at (insert awesome breakfast place here) on Fridays before work. I'll spring for breakfast. What do you think?" Then be silent and let him respond.

If your children do not respond initially, start the study without them. If this is new to you, they are probably having trouble reconciling what you said to your past behavior. They will watch to see if you are serious or if this is just a passing fancy. Remember in Chapter Two we said that the best thing you can do for your kids is to walk with God personally. Doing this study is one way for you to do that.

If your kids are younger, they will probably think it is a great deal to get some time alone with you. The fact of the matter is, it is. You are essential to your children's development as people and believers. There may need to be some rearrangement of schedules to accommodate the new activity together, but it will be worth whatever accommodations you have to make.

If there is resistance from the younger children, move the scale of the invitation toward what is described above for the older children.

Your Enemy's Commitment

Mark 4:13–20 says, "And He said to them, "Do you not understand this parable? How will you understand all the parables? The sower sows the word. 'These are the ones who are beside the road where the word is sown; and when they hear, immediately **Satan** comes and takes away the word which has been sown in them. In a similar way these are the ones on whom seed was sown on the rocky places, who, when they hear the word, immediately receive it with joy; and they have no firm root in themselves, but are only temporary; then, when **affliction or persecution** arises because of the word, immediately they fall away. And others are the ones on whom seed was sown among the thorns; these are the ones who have heard the word, but the **worries of the world, and the deceitfulness of riches, and the desires for other things** enter in and choke the word, and it becomes unfruitful. And those are the ones on whom seed was sown on the good soil; and they hear the word and accept it and bear fruit, thirty, sixty, and a hundredfold." (Emphasis added.)

Note that Mark tells us that when we are dealing with the Word of God, we have resistance from the enemy. That resistance takes at least three forms. Let's look at them in reverse order.

Distraction

The first method the enemy uses to take away the Word of God from us is distraction. Mark describes the distraction as worries, deceitfulness, and desires. Working on this book has been a real struggle. There have been many things that have cropped up to distract me from the goal of finishing this, and in some cases, even starting it. Some of the distractions were good opportunities. I was offered the choice to either slug through this project or take another route that would provide immediate solutions for some of the challenges we were facing as a family. At the same time, a key event for which I had been planning was canceled. I was discouraged — really discouraged. We had seemed to build up momentum in the ministry, and we were being shut down. Not only shut down, but we also were literally pulled away from the vision of what we understood God wanted us to do.

One morning I was talking this over with the Lord, and He directed me to Psalm 27:4. That is the first verse I ever memorized as a new believer. In the New American Standard it says: "One thing I have asked from the Lord, that I shall seek: That I may dwell in the house of the Lord all the days of my life, to behold the beauty of the Lord and to meditate in His temple." In verse eight David writes, "When You said, 'Seek My face,' my heart said to You, 'Your face, O Lord, I shall seek.' " I was struck by the word *seek* in these verses. I pulled my concordance off the shelf and looked at the verses that had *seek* in relation to the Lord in the Old Testament. I found that there were two primary roots and thought that was interesting, but more interesting was a phrase that I found repeated with these words several times, *set your heart*. I saw this four times in Chronicles[1]. It reminded me of Ezra 7:10: "For Ezra had set his heart to study the law of the Lord and to practice it, and to teach His statutes and ordinances in Israel."

If you are like me, you have set your heart on a lot of things. You set your heart on a new car, a house, graduation for your child, retirement, and success in business or ministry. However, it is not on those things that we are directed to set our hearts. We are to set our hearts to seek the face of Christ. That is the measure of success. In the movie *City Slickers*, Jack Palance's character, Curly, has this exchange with Billy Crystal's Mitch:

> *Curly: Do you know what the secret of life is?*
> *[holds up one finger]*
> *Curly: This.*
> *Mitch: Your finger?*

---

[1] 1 Chronicles 22:19; Chronicles 11:16; 2 Chronicles 12:14; 2 Chronicles 19:3

> *Curly: One thing. Just one thing. You stick to that,*
> *and the rest don't mean shit.*
> *Mitch: But, what is the "one thing?"*
> *Curly: [smiles] That's what **you** have to find out.*[2]

The one thing is what Psalm 27:4 identifies for us. Seeking God is what is important. Jesus reiterates this in Matthew 6:33: "But seek first His kingdom and His righteousness, and all these things will be added to you." He tells us in the context of this verse that the *all* we typically set our hearts on, He will provide. We need to seek Him.

But the enemy will try to distract us with worries, riches, and desires for other things. We are inundated daily with claims on our time and our money. We are told that we have to have the latest and/or greatest of everything in order to have a fulfilled life. But the reality is that we just need to seek His face. The rest is noise that will distract us from what we really need to be doing.

I am not suggesting here that we go out to the wilderness, find a tree, sit down, and check out. But I am suggesting that we have to fight for the time we need with the Lord. Setting our minds does not conjure up images of a casual approach or something that will happen without effort. It seems to me, and it is my experience, that we have to work at getting the time we need to focus on Him. Further, it is my experience that when we sit down to enter into that time of "seeking," all hell breaks loose. I do not know what your experience may be, but when I sit down and try to get quiet, my mind starts racing with all of the things I have

---

[2] *City Slickers.* Director Ron Underwood, Castle Rock Entertainment. Beverly Hills, CA. MGM Home Entertainment, 2008, DVD Recording.

Resistance to Implementation

to do — bills, projects, ideas for the next great mousetrap, alarm at whether the hose is rolled up and out of the weather. You know, important stuff. But it comes like a flood. This is exacerbated by one of my strategies for dealing with life. I am an idea guy, and I use ideas and thinking as a way to gain acceptance and approval from people. So when an idea that seems good comes, I feel compelled to capture it so I can use it later. The enemy knows this. As I mentioned in Chapter Three, I am learning that when I sit down to meet with the Lord, the enemy will flood me with good ideas, even ideas about how to promote my ministry or deal with issues that have come up for the men with whom I am meeting. While all of that is good, it is not the best. It distracts me from what is needed at the time, seeking the face of my Lord. I have had to learn to let all of that stuff — all of that noise, all of that distraction, even the good stuff — go. I have had to learn to trust God that if the things that are coming at me during that time are important, He will bring them back to my mind when and if I need to act on them.

The enemy may not try to distract you with ideas; that may not be your hot button. But, he knows what it is and will use it. The key is to work through the distractions and set your mind to meet with your Father in the Word.

Affliction and Persecution

One of the things that the Lord has allowed me to do is to serve Youth With a Mission in Trinidad and Tobago. I have taught on their base four times. I did the first "Fathers to Sons" workshop with the staff. In the Discipleship Training School, I have taught three times; once on how to do Bible study and twice on the nature and character of God. We study the nature and character of God for five days while we backpack through a rainforest along the northern coast of the island. This trip has been during the rainy season for the past two years. We have a blast. Apart from the sand fleas, it is incredible. The forest is dense and amazing in its diversity of plant life. Coconuts, almonds, mango, papaya, coco, and oranges are abundant. There are other sources of food everywhere. The trees are immense, and there is one tree that is particularly striking. I do not know the name of it, but it has a massively extensive root system. The tree reaches hundreds of feet into the air and clings to the side of very steep terrain. The circumference is such that ten of us would not be able to encircle the tree. The roots literally start ten to twenty feet above the ground and radiate like the arms of some huge octopus down at 30 to 45 degree angles into and along the ground. Everywhere we walk in the forest, we are stepping on or over these roots. They are literally holding the island together in that part of the forest. I have pictures of one of the students standing between two of the massive roots. In the picture, he is dwarfed by them, and you cannot see the entire diameter of the tree.

The island has endured storms and hurricanes for centuries, but these trees are unfazed by all that these storms can throw at them. They have stood through them all. Why have they been able to withstand that type of affliction? From observation and from our passage here in Mark, we learn that it is because they have massive root systems. It has taken many years — time — to create these root systems. These trees have dug deep into the soil of the island, and they have sought the nutrients there to cause the growth of these enormous trees. They are not an overnight sensation, but decades in the making.

In Philippians 1:27 – 29, Paul tells us that if we are following Christ we can expect that we will have opponents. He tells us that we do not need to be alarmed by them. Then he substantiates his encouragement by telling us that we have been granted the privilege of suffering for Christ. While that is not something I would choose as encouragement, it is instructive. If we are going to attempt to live out this Christian life, especially in the arena of sharing life with others, including our kids, we will have affliction and persecution. If we have not taken the time to sink roots deep into the Word, we will not withstand this onslaught. Like the tree, it will take time for us to develop these roots. This is counter to our culture because we are accustomed to things being finished quickly. But to extend roots takes time, reflection, meditation, and work.

Jeremiah 17:8 echoes this theme, "For he will be like a tree planted by the water, That extends its roots by a stream And will not fear when the heat comes; But its leaves will be green, And it will not be anxious in a year of drought Nor cease to yield fruit." And Psalm 1:2-3 tells us how we are to develop these roots, "But his delight is in the law of the Lord, And in His law he meditates day and night. He will be like a tree firmly planted by streams of water, Which yields its fruit in its season And its leaf does not wither; And in whatever he does, he prospers." Note in order to develop roots in the Word, we have to spend time in it.

Satan Takes Away the Word

The first thing that Christ says happens with the Word when it is sown is the enemy comes to take it away. In most of the Christian communities with which I have been associated, not much is said about the enemy coming after us. However, this notion of having to fight him and his minions permeates scripture. It is beyond the scope of this book to go into a full treatment of spiritual warfare[3], but it is a reality we face daily as we try to walk with God. He hates the Word of God and Christ says he will come after it. How do we deal with this? James 4:7–8 tells us how, "Submit therefore to God. Resist the devil and he will flee from you. Draw near to God and He will draw near to you. Cleanse your hands, you sinners; and purify your hearts, you double-minded."

There are three steps here. First we have to realize that the enemy is coming after us. This will not be an overt attack, but rather in the form of subtle suggestions like: "This will never work." "You can't do this." "Your daughter will not be interested in this." "Others may be able to do this, but you can't." Those thoughts are coming from the enemy. They are not something that the Holy Spirit would say to you. So what do we do?

The next step according to James is to submit to God. That means we acknowledge His Lordship and sovereignty over our lives and do what he says rather than what the enemy says. We also acknowledge His victory over the enemy. I do not know a better way to do this than in prayer. Before God, acknowledge the obstacle and how it makes you feel, and tell Him that you are submitting yourself to Him rather than the suggestions of the enemy. For example if you are hearing, "This will never work," you might pray something like this:

---

[3] If you are interested in learning more about this topic, I would suggest Ed Murphy's work, *The Handbook for Spiritual Warfare*. It is a thorough treatment of the subject from a biblical, theological, and practical point of view by one who is a scholar and a missionary with field experience.

Father, I am struggling with discouragement. I want to get into your Word and share the experience with my son. I am hearing that it will not work. Your Word says that it is living and active and sharper than any two-edged sword and that it will not return void. Lord, I submit myself to you and to your Word over and against this discouragement that is being thrown against me by the enemy.

That is the start, but you are not done yet. The third part of what James recommends is to resist the devil. We are to do this. It is our battle to fight. Remember what we said through our investigation of Ephesians 6? We are to take up the full armor of God every day. So you may want to finish your prayer against discouragement like this:

In the name of Jesus Christ, I rebuke this spirit of discouragement and bind you to the feet of Christ for judgment. I claim the blood of Christ on this effort to grow deep in the Word of God and the dominion of Christ over any attempt to discourage or distract me from seeking Christ in His Word.

Moving ourselves to apply what we have been talking about will be resisted by the enemy. But through the life, death, burial, resurrection, and ascension of our Lord, the enemy has been defeated, and we have been given the means to resist and overcome him. We are told that we are responsible to resist, so that resistance becomes a matter of obedience for us.

Persistence

There is at least one other thing that will keep you from being successful in building into the lives of your children — failure. What you try at first may not work.

One final encouragement — persist. Not all that you try to do with your children will work. Each one of them is an individual. But you keep trying. Proverbs 24:16 tells us, "For a righteous man falls seven times, and rises again, But the wicked stumble in time of calamity." It is a fact of life that we will fail at some of the things that we attempt. I mentioned earlier that in our workshops, my sons are interviewed by the men. One of the things that has come out time and time again is that we did things with them that they did not like. Some of the forms of family devotions we tried were not received all that well. So we regrouped and tried something else.

You have to keep trying, persisting. By that I am not saying that you ram the Word down the kids' throats, but you keep trying different things to help them understand the Word. To paraphrase Mother Teresa, "What you try to get your children in the Word may not work at first; try anyway."

While our kids were living at home, we ate a lot of meals together. Jenny worked hard to make sure that we could sit down together as a family as often as possible. Hanging in a prominent place where we eat is a framed picture. Well, it really is a motivational poster that was hanging in the break room at the place I worked during our stint in seminary. It is a print of a Norman Rockwell picture. There is a man who is obviously a clerk leaning over what appears to be a cracker barrel. Behind him on the walls are several pictures of Abraham Lincoln. He is reading a law book that is propped up on another law book that has several book- marks sticking out. There is yet another law book on the floor next to him. There is a look of rapt concentration on his face, and the caption under the picture is "Perseverance Precedes Excellence." That is what it takes. Perseverance.

CHAPTER 9
Final Word

A Path Forward

Launch into this yourself. As we said at the beginning of our time together, this is not about getting it right. This is about getting to know Jesus and bringing your sons (and daughters) along with you on the journey.

Present it that way to them. Do not take on the burden of being the expert or having to have all the answers before you get started. Just admit to yourself and them that you are not omniscient, but you know One who is. Then just dive in.

Do not force this either. If you feel that you need more time on a particular book, give yourself permission to take the time. I would encourage you to meet regularly with your kids regardless of whether you have finished the study. It solidifies the habit and helps protect the time you have set aside for them.

Resources

One of the things I tell the men who come to my workshops is that I am committed to them for life. I offer to meet with them whenever they want to go over this. That offer stands for you as well with some modifications.

Handbook

As mentioned in the introduction, there is a companion workbook to this book. It would be a great way for you to get started. The workbook is designed to give you a place to do the studies we covered and give you a point of comparison.

In the workshops my biggest role is to remove barriers between men and the Word of God. That is done primarily by being a cheerleader for them. It is not hard. The reality is this: if you get into the Word for yourself, the Lord shows up. He wants to meet with you. At the workshops, time and time again, men with no formal Bible training open the Word and follow the steps outlined in this book. They see the same things in 2 Peter that the men who write the commentaries and notes in the men's study Bibles saw and more.

Do you remember the first Matrix movie? Remember after the fight scene in the Dojo, Morpheus had Tank upload the jump program[1]. As Neo and Morpheus stood on the top of a skyscraper, Morpheus told Neo that in order to jump from one building to the next he had to, "Free your mind." That's what you need to do to make this jump. You do not need commentaries. Your study Bible is keeping you from dependence on the Holy Spirit. Free your mind from thinking you need someone to make sure you pulled the right stuff out of scripture. Make the leap. Meet with God.

---

[1] *The Matrix*. Director Andy Wachowski, Warner Brothers Pictures, Burbank, CA. Warner Brothers, 2009, DVD Recording.

Website

As mentioned several times throughout this book, there is a page set up for you on the Entrusting Truth website to download materials. The page is not part of the navigation of the site, thus you have to have the URL to get there, and it is: http://entrustingtruth.org/index.cfm?id = 68. That period is the end of the sentence, not part of the URL. Type the URL into the address field of your browser and then hit enter. Some of the things you will find there:

- Catechism for Young Children

- Files to Study in Word:
  1 John 1
  2 Peter

- Other resources will be added.

On the website you will also find my blog. If you sign up on the site, I will notify you when the blog is updated. It is not set up for RSS at the moment. I will send you an email when we update it, and it will have part of the blog post and a link to read the rest. We do not share your E-mail address with anyone.

Workshops

The workshops Entrusting Truth conducts have been mentioned several times throughout the book. These are typically four-and-a-half hour workshops that are done on a Saturday morning. During that time, I walk the men through the process of doing the book overview.

If you would like to schedule a workshop for your group, there is information on the website explaining the process.

Me

Finally, there is me. If you have any questions or thoughts about this, you are more than welcome to contact me. There is contact information on the website.

Dive in. You, your wife, and your children will be eternally grateful that you did.

CHAPTER 10
Sons' Responses

Questions

At the end of the workshops we do, some or all of my sons come and are interviewed by the men. The following are some of the questions they have asked and the answers given.

I have pulled some of these answers directly from audio recordings of the workshops. I also pulled all of the questions from the audio and provided them to my sons John, Jeff, and Brian. Some of the answers below are written responses to the questions.

At this point John is 28, married to Morgan and expecting their first child in August of 2010. John is a C.P.A. and helps lead worship at the church they attend. Morgan is on staff at that church as the connections coordinator, and helps people find ministries in which they can be involved and coordinates weddings.

Jeff is 24 and in his second year of medical school. Brian is 21 and has started in the architecture program at Oklahoma State University.

How has this impacted your life?

Jeff: It has changed the way I do Bible study. I seem to get more out of the studies that I do.

John: It has given me a good system of how to study the Bible, which has really helped me in understanding scripture. Morgan and I have had a turbulent last year and a half or two years and just having a better overall understanding of scripture has really helped me through that. Morgan's brother was killed about a year and a half ago; having a better grasp of the scriptures has been very helpful in dealing with that.

How has this affected your spiritual journey?

Jeff: I feel like I learn more about God when I employ this technique. Learning more about God makes me feel like I have grown closer to Him as well.

Brian: I get into the Bible more because I have a structured time to do it. When I was younger, I did not do a daily Bible study in high school, but now I have started studying the Bible. All the Old Testament stuff...well, before I couldn't tell you anything about it. But now I can do that a lot better.

John: I had the benefit of being first. It has been great for me. Sometimes I will have had a hard week at work, and I will show up not totally ready. We will spend half the time talking about something else. Politics, football, still there is a value there building a relationship with my dad. We talk, and we hang out together.

Like Brian said, before we did this I had done the fill-in-the-blank Bible studies, where you go to Mardel and pick out a book. It's like, "hey, read these six verses, fill in the blanks"; those are great. But they don't really do much for me personally. This has really helped me out. We finished the New Testament before Brian started. Before we did that if you had asked me, "What is Romans about?" "Hey, what is Galatians about?" I had no idea.

Going through this for most of the books of the New Testament, I feel like I have a decent handle on just the general idea. I am not anywhere near a scholar or anything like that, but it has made me feel more comfortable in my faith. It has really helped my relationship with God because when you are in His Word, you are hearing from Him on a weekly basis. (I interjected here that John had done Bible studies in college; he led them on his floor in the dorm.) This system works really well for me, and it helps me get the big picture. This gives me the overall story arc, and then I can break it down into components and study them.

How has it affected your relationship with your dad?

Brian: It definitely improved it. It opened more doors to be able to communicate with him, just to relate to him better. It has definitely strengthened our relationship, I think. It is a lot easier to talk to him about things that I wanted or needed.

John: One thing that I think was good — it helped move the relationship. It made the relationship less hierarchical and more of an equal. Not that I... I have a great amount of respect for my dad. (Lots of laughter breaks out in the room). It helped transition that relationship; I am not a child anymore.... I am an adult, and the relationship changes a little; this has helped that.

Why did you want to do this with your dad?

Jeff: I wanted to do this with my dad because I knew that he knew how to study the Bible and knew a lot about the Bible. Another reason that I wanted to join him is that I knew with him I would not get someone just telling me I need to study the Bible, but would get some substance and learn how to study the Bible. I found that the church seemed to do more of the telling you to study the Bible, but tends to avoid the substance, which is really frustrating.

John: Right after I graduated from college, I realized that I didn't really have a great grasp of the overall story of the Bible. I knew that my dad did, so I asked him if we could start going through it.

What do you remember from when you were young? What are the key take-aways from time with your dad?

Brian: They did not do the crayon Bible study thing with me. We have these really large story books. They would read those to me, and we would talk about what it meant. There was some other stuff. It is a really cool book that had big pictures.[1]

John: A key take-away for me was that the Bible was important. They kept trying different things to get us in the Bible. In high school they did family church on Sunday afternoons. They would say, "OK, everyone down to the living room. We are going to have family worship." That was lame. I would be in the middle of a video game, and they would make me turn it off. I did not like it, but it communicated that it was more important than what I was doing. It underlined the importance of the Bible. I remember doing memory verses at the dining room table, going through the catechism in a "Mother-may-I" format, reading from the big picture Bible story books.

---

[1] Ella K. Lindvall, *Read Aloud Bible Stories, Vol. 1,* (Chicago: Moody Press, 1982). Volumes 2, 3, and 4 are the same publisher 1985, 1990, and 1995 respectively. These books are available on my website. Note these are referenced earlier on page 107 of the manuscript it is redundant here but this will help clarity.

What do you like about doing this?

Jeff: It challenges me to get my stuff done beforehand and be prepared for Bible study. I also like the different inputs from my brothers and dad.

John: It really helps me to stay consistent in my time in the Word and helps provide structure to that time.

Why would you do this with your dad?

Jeff: Because he actually teaches how to do Bible study as opposed to just telling me to do it. Also, he provides insight and wisdom that I cannot get anywhere else. I felt like it would be an extreme waste of a resource if I did not try to pick my dad's brain as he went to seminary.

John: Because he knows what he is talking about.

What do your meetings usually look like? Do you always do the study? Is this accountability?

Jeff: We intro with what we did from the Bible study usually starting with summaries. Then we will go into what we got out of the passage. We do not always study; sometimes we talk about sports, frustrations with work/school, or politics. This usually occurs when someone was unable to prepare for the study due to a busy week. I do not think of this as accountability; I think of this as a Bible study. I mean we talk about each other's week, but the main focus is the Bible study and what God is revealing in this passage.

John: We usually meet for breakfast. We usually talk about other stuff that is going on for about 30 minutes and then transition into talking about the Bible study. No, we don't always talk about the Bible study. If one or both of us aren't ready, sometimes we just talk about sports or life, etc.

Did you already know how to do this when you started with your dad? Particularly the outlining of the passages?

Jeff: I had previously asked my dad how to do a Bible study, and he had taught me this method. So, yeah, I knew, but my dad still had to teach me again.

John: I knew how to outline something, however, I had not applied the process to Bible study, and I did not know a lot of the structural things to look for specifically.

Did it you take you three hours to do the study the first time?

Jeff: Probably pretty close to that. I do not remember when my dad invited me to join the Bible study, but I believe that it was on one of the larger books. Plus it was just the night before that I was invited. But even after that it probably took me close to two or three hours each time to do a good job.

John: I honestly don't remember. I seem to think it took a little longer than that.

Do you do this with anyone else?

Jeff: So far I have not.

John: My wife, Morgan, and I have gone through a couple of books together. It is something that we need to do better at — studying the Bible together. I meet with a member of the Sunday school class that I am a member of once a week, and we use a slightly modified version of this format.

John: I do this with a guy in my Sunday school class. There is a different dynamic when you are doing it with someone who is at the same level of maturity as you are. It is more of a sharing. I think if you approach it that way with your kids, especially kids in high school, you could help them get into it more. The way my wife and I do it, we outline the book separately. Then come in and talk about it. My wife works at a church and can do Bible study during the day.

How long have you been doing this with your dad?

Jeff: I did it for about a year then went to med school.

Brian: I started when I was a freshman in college. I am a junior now, so about a year and a half.

John: Almost three years.

Was there a trigger point that made you want to know more about the Bible?

Jeff: During high school when I became frustrated with the church because all they were doing was telling me that I should study the Bible. The church, in my opinion, has failed to teach people how to study the Bible.

John: In college when I was away from home, I was exposed to a lot of different things. It was then that I made my faith my own. I was having a period of introspection, and I thought I do not really know what this book I have been carrying around since I was five even says. I tried to do it on my own a couple of times, but I did not make it past Leviticus. The Old Testament was boring so I would go to Romans and get lost in Paul's arguments. I would think, "What is he talking about?" Then I would study a short book. I did not have a good system for doing this. What working with my dad has done is help me find a good system for studying the Bible that helps me build a structure in my mind for what a book is about. If I know what the books are about, I know what the testaments are about, and then what the whole story is about.

Brian: For me the consistency of being surrounded by things about God. As I said earlier, they would always try different things; they would try one thing, and if it did not work, they would try something else. They would take me to church events like small group and different activities. After a while it was like John said, I just did not know what the Bible said. I would not be able to have a conversation about it with someone. So, yeah, I guess it is a maturity thing.

John: I did not own it till college, but all the things my mom and dad did while growing up.... I would not have known where to start in life without that.

What age were you when you had a desire to learn on your own?

John: Second year of college.

Brian: Second semester of my senior year in high school. (Clarifying question: Was it because of peer influence?) Well, I am from Jenks, and I really did not like a lot of the things they did so I just.... Jenks and Union are kind of similar in the atmospheres, but there was just a lot of stuff they were doing that I was not interested in. I was looking for something else. I also went to Young Life, Trail West as work crew. I also did mission trips to Bangkok and Trinidad.

Did you ever feel like your dad was preaching at you?

Jeff: Nope. The way it usually worked was my dad asked us questions with the expectation that we would be prepared and have thought about it. His questions were intended to provoke thought, but not to preach at us. I would think, "Man. My dad's better at this than me."

John: Every once in a while, but not very often.

How do we keep our kids out of trouble?

Brian: Encourage them to be involved with their church. That is what they (mom and dad) did. Mom was not OK with me going to Bangkok when I first told her about it, but eventually she was OK with it. They encouraged me to do mission trips, to be involved in the youth groups.

John: (In response to a comment that there are gaps in the interest and growth of kids) One of the things was what they did before we hit the gap. When we started going to our current church, I got plugged into the youth group in the seventh grade. I got plugged in to a small group that really helped me a lot through high school and even into college a little bit. The leader, during high school, I would have probably talked to him before I talked to my parents. He was on my parent's team, and I did not know it. They had me set up in that relationship and had me going down that path before I was at the point where I was like, "My parents are idiots."

Do you have time to do this in med school or work?

Jeff: Until recently I had not done this while in medical school or undergrad school for that matter. I realized while I was talking in one of these groups for my dad, that I was being hypocritical telling people that this Bible study should be used and not doing it myself. So starting at about halfway through my second semester first year, I began to employ this method for my own personal Bible study. I do it every morning while eating breakfast. I am about to break the outline up into three days, then I do about two verses per day. It is not much, but I have been able to get a pretty good Bible study on Ephesians. I am going to move on to a new book soon.

John: Yes.

How has it changed your relationship with your dad?

Jeff: I have always gone to my dad for spiritual advice and questions, and I think this has changed it by making it more frequent.

How do you get teenagers interested in this?

Brian: I did not do this in high school; I do not know if I would have wanted to. I couldn't because of schedule (Brian was in band and had to be at the band room at 0600 each morning.) Dad did not say, "Hey we are going to do this Bible study." He took that approach earlier in our life (laughs). We had like family church after church and that was a terrible idea. Dad just told me what he and John were doing and said I could join them if I wanted to. John asked me to join them too. There were a lot of times if we weren't ready, we wouldn't do it. Like if John or I were not ready, we would just talk. It was really casual, not like, "Have you guys done your homework?" or whatever.

Jeff: I liked the breakfast.

Brian: One way would be to make it clear that you are not preaching to them, because that is not what this is at all.

John: I wasn't interested when I was a teenager. However, my parents were really good about finding allies that I was interested in spending time with, in my case a small group leader at our church.

What do you think you will do with your kids?

John: We will probably work through similar types of study with them. Starting small with snippets of scripture and Bible memorization and moving into more in-depth study as they have the capacity for it.

What was the advantage of doing this together, rather than on your own?

Jeff: You get different perspectives.

John: I worked in accounting for a couple of years while we were doing this, and from January to April, I was not ready some mornings. It was cool because we talked about sports or football as we had breakfast. We talked about my work.

Is it uncomfortable for you to answer these questions?

John: Not really.

Brian: No, I am used to being in front of crowds.

Jeff: Brian's a pretty big deal... (audio obliterated by laughter)

Appendices

I have said throughout the book that observation is not only the essential place to start in studying the Bible, but also the key to everything else you do in the study. The following story focuses on the importance of observation.

"In the Laboratory with Agassiz," by Samuel H. Scudder[1]

It was more than fifteen years ago that I entered the laboratory of Professor Agassiz, and told him I had enrolled my name in the Scientific School as a student of natural history. He asked me a few questions about my object in coming, my antecedents generally,[1] the mode in which I afterwards proposed to use the knowledge I might acquire,

[1] Lee Archie and John G. Archie, "Reading for Philosophical Inquiry: A Brief Introduction to Philosophical Thinking" ver. 0.21; An Open Source Reader, Chapter 2. "The Nature of Learning: Recognition of Different Perspectives"; available from http://philosophy.lander.edu/intro/introbook2.1/x426.html; accessed 28 August 2005.

and, finally, whether I wished to study any special branch. To the latter I replied that, while I wished to be well grounded in all departments of zoology, I purposed to devote myself specially to insects.

"When do you wish to begin?" he asked.

"Now," I replied.

This seemed to please him, and with an energetic "Very well!" he reached from a shelf a huge jar of specimens in yellow alcohol. "Take this fish," he said, "and look at it; we call it a haemulon; by and by I will ask what you have seen."

With that he left me, but in a moment returned with explicit instructions as to the care of the object entrusted to me.

"No man is fit to be a naturalist," said he, "who does not know how to take care of specimens."

I was to keep the fish before me in a tin tray, and occasionally moisten the surface with alcohol from the jar, always taking care to replace the stopper tightly. Those were not the days of ground-glass stoppers and elegantly shaped exhibition jars; all the old students will recall the huge neckless glass bottles with their leaky, wax-besmeared corks, half eaten by insects, and begrimed with cellar dust. Entomology was a cleaner science than ichthyology, but the example of the Professor, who had unhesitatingly plunged to the bottom of the jar to produce the fish, was infectious; and though this alcohol had a "very ancient and fishlike smell," I really dared not show any aversion within these sacred precincts, and treated the alcohol as though it were pure water. Still I was conscious of a passing feeling of disappointment, for gazing at a fish did not commend itself to an ardent entomologist. My friends at home, too, were annoyed when they discovered that no amount of eau-de-Cologne would drown the perfume which haunted me like a shadow.

In ten minutes I had seen all that could be seen in that fish, and started in search of the Professor—who had, however, left the Museum; and when I returned, after lingering over some of the odd animals stored in the upper apartment, my specimen was dry all over. I dashed the fluid over the fish as if to resuscitate the beast from a fainting fit, and looked with anxiety for a return of the normal sloppy appearance. This little excitement over, nothing was to be done but to return to a steadfast gaze at my mute companion. Half an hour passes—an hour—another hour; the fish began to look loathsome. I turned it over and around; looked it in the face—ghastly; from behind, beneath, above, sideways, at a three-quarter's view—just as ghastly. I was in despair; at an early hour I concluded that lunch was necessary; so, with infinite relief, the fish was carefully replaced in the jar, and for an hour I was free.

On my return, I learned that Professor Agassiz had been at the Museum, but had gone, and would not return for several hours. My fellow students were too busy to be disturbed by continued conversation. Slowly I drew forth that hideous fish, and with a feeling of desperation again looked at it. I might not use a magnifying-glass; instruments of all kinds were interdicted. My two hands, my two eyes, and the fish: it seemed a most limited field. I pushed my finger down its throat to feel how sharp the teeth were. I began to count the scales in the *different rows, until I was convinced that that was nonsense. At last a happy thought struck me—I would draw the fish; and now with surprise I began to discover new features in the creature. Just then the Professor returned.*

"That is right," said he: "a pencil is one of the best of eyes. I am glad to notice, too, that you kept your specimen wet, and your bottle corked."

With these encouraging words, he added, "Well, what is it like?"

He listened attentively to my brief rehearsal of the structure of parts whose names were still unknowns to me: the fringed gill-arches and movable operculum; the pores of the head, fleshy lips and lidless eyes; the lateral line, the spinous fins and forked tail; the compressed and arched body. When I finished, he waited as if expecting more, and then, with an air of disappointment, "You have not looked very carefully; why," he continued more earnestly, "you haven't even seen one of the most conspicuous features of the animal, which is a plainly before your eyes as the fish itself; look again, look again!" and he left me to my misery.

I was piqued; I was mortified. Still more of that wretched fish! But now I set myself to my tasks with a will, and discovered on new thing after another, until I saw how just the Professor's criticism had been. The afternoon passed quickly; and when, towards its close, the Professor inquired, "Do you see it yet?"

"No," I replied, "I am certain I do not, but I see how little I saw before."

"That is next best," said he, earnestly, "but I won't hear you now; put away your fish and go home;

perhaps you will be ready with a better answer in the morning. I will examine you before you look at the fish."

This was disconcerting. Not only must I think of my fish all night, studying, without the object before me, what this unknown but most visible feature might be; but also, without reviewing my discoveries, I must give an exact account of them the next day. I had a bad memory, so I walked home by Charles River in a distracted state, with my two perplexities.

The cordial greeting from the Professor the next morning was reassuring; here was a man who seemed to be quite as anxious as I that I should see for myself what he saw.

"Do you perhaps mean," I asked, "that the fish has symmetrical sides with paired organs?"

His thoroughly pleased "Of course! of course!" repaid the wakeful hours of the previous night. After he had discoursed most happily and enthusiastically—as he always did—upon the importance of this point, I ventured to ask what I should do next.

"Oh, look at your fish!" he said, and left me again to my own devices. In a little more than an hour he returned, and heard my new catalogue.

"That is good, that is good!" he repeated, "but that is not all; go on"; and so for three long days he placed that fish before my eyes, forbidding me to look at anything else, or to use any artificial aid. "Look, look, look," was his repeated injunction.

This was the best entomological lesson I ever had— a lesson whose influence has extended to the details of every subsequent study; a legacy the Professor had left to me, as he has left it to many others, of inestimable value, which we could not buy, with which we cannot part.

A year afterward, some of us were amusing ourselves with chalking outlandish beasts on the Museum blackboard. We drew prancing starfishes; frogs in mortal combat; hydra-headed worms; stately crawfishes, standing on their tails, bearing aloft umbrellas; and grotesque fishes with gaping mouths and staring eyes. The Professor came in shortly after, and was as amused as any at our experiments. he looked at the fishes.

"Haemulons, every one of them," he said; "Mr. — drew them."

True; and to this day, if I attempt a fish, I can draw nothing but haemulons.

The fourth day, a second fish of the same group was placed beside the first, and I was bidden to point out the resemblances and differences between the two; another and another followed, until the entire family lay before me, and a whole legion of jars covered the table and surrounding shelves; the odor had become a pleasant perfume; and even now, the sight of an old, six-inch, worm-eaten cork brings fragrant memories.

The whole group of haemulons was thus brought in review; and, whether engaged upon the dissection of the internal organs, the preparation and examination of the bony framework, or the description of the various parts, Agassiz's training in the method of observing facts and their orderly arrangement was ever accompanied by the urgent exhortation not to be content with them.

"Facts are stupid things," he would say, "until brought into connection with some general law."

At the end of eight months, it was almost with reluctance that I left these friends and turned to insects; but what I had gained by this outside experience has been of greater value than years of later investigation in my favorite groups.[2]

[1] Ed. These "antecedents" as elaborated by another former student of Agassiz may be of interest. (We sometimes underestimate the educational processes of the past by comparison with our own.) Professor Shaler writes "The examination Agassiz gave me was directed first to find that I knew enough Latin and Greek to make use of those languages; that I could patter a little of them evidently pleased him. He didn't care for those detestable rules for scanning. Then came German and French, which were also approved: I could read both, and spoke the former fairly well. He did not probe me in my weakest place, mathematics, for the good reason that, badly as I was off in that subject, he was in a worse plight. Then asking me concerning my reading, he found that I had read the Essay on Classification, and had noted in it the influence of Schelling's views. Most of his questioning related to this field, and the more than fair beginning of our relations then made was due to the fact that I had some enlargement on that side. So, too, he was pleased to find that I had managed a lot of Latin, Greek, and German poetry, and had been trained with the sword. He completed this inquiry by requiring that I bring

my foils and masks for a bout." Nathaniel Southgate Shaler, The Autobiography of Nathaniel Southgate Shaler, Boston, MA: Houghton Mifflin, 1907, 93-100.

[2] *Samuel H. Scudder, "In the Laboratory With Agassiz", Every Saturday, (April 4, 1974) 16, 369-370.*

Chart Instructions

1. On the chart draw lines vertically to show your divisions for the book. If you have four divisions, you would draw lines to create four divisions as shown below.

Jonah			

Section Title	Section Title	Section Title	Section Title
Start verse - end	Start verse - end	Start verse - end	Start verse - end
Short description of what happens in this section	Short description of what happens in this section	Short description of what happens in this section	Short description of what happens in this section

KeyVerse :

Application

Themes:

2. Put the verses for your divisions on the second line of blocks created by the lines. (Start verse – end verse above)

3. Put a short description of the passage in the big box.

4. Put a title that captures your understanding of each section at the top of each section. The titles should be short and memorable. (Section Title above)

5. Title the book in five words or less. Make it something that you will remember that captures what the book is about; be creative. (NOT JONAH above)

Annotated Bibliography

Books About How to Do Bible Study

Henrichsen, Walter A. *A Layman's Guide to Interpreting the Bible.* Grand Rapids, MI: Zondervan Publishing House. Colorado Springs: Navpress, 1978.

> This book has good simple principles on how to interpret scripture in a consistent manner.

Henrichsen, Walter A. *Understand.* With a Foreword by Robert D. Foster. Colorado Springs: Navpress, 1976.

> This is a shorter earlier version of the previous book.

Jensen, Irving L. *Independent Bible Study.* Chicago: Moody Press, 1963.

> This is a very good how-to manual. The key contribution of Jensen to synthetic Bible study is his charting methodology.

Lincoln, William C. *Personal Bible Study.* Minneapolis: Bethany Fellowship, Inc., 1975.

Search the Scriptures. Colorado Springs: Navpress, 1974.

> Simple how-to book used by thousands in doing chapter and book analysis study.

Tenney, Merrill C. *Galatians the Charter of Christian Liberty.* Grand Rapids, MI: Wm. B. Eerdmans Publishing Co., 1950.

This is a good example of how a synthetic study is done. It has the further advantage of being a good commentary on Galatians.

The Navigator Bible Studies Handbook. Colorado Springs: Navpress, 1979.

This is a manual of how to do several different types of Bible study.

Traina, Robert A. *Methodical Bible Study.* Wilmore, KY: By the Author, Asbury Theological Seminary, 1952.

This is the root text for most of the works on Bible study. Traina's work is the best on the subject. He is a bit odd when it comes to application. However, his insights on how to better observe, interpret, and correlate with other scripture are invaluable. This is a standard seminary text-book. It may be hard to locate. I would try Christian Book Distributors (http://www.christianbook.com/) or similar sources. Recently, I have found that Amazon is a great resource for old books through their re-seller network. Or just do an internet search.

Vos, Howard F. Vos. *Effective Bible Study: A Guide to Sixteen Methods.* Grand Rapids: Zondervan Publishing House, 1970.

Warren, Rick. *Personal Bible Study Methods.* By the author, 1981.

Wald, Oletta. *The Joy of Discovery in Bible Study, Revised Edition.* Minneapolis: Augsburg Printing House, 1975.

This is one of Traina's disciples. She attempts, success-fully, to get the hay out of the loft and down to the level of most readers. It is particularly good on observation.

Books About or Models of Synthetic Bible Study

All of these books are the product of synthetic Bible study. They treat the books as wholes.

Baxter, J. Sidlow. *Explore the Book: A Basic and Broadly Interpretive Course of Bible Study from Genesis to Revelation.* Grand Rapids, Zondervan Publishing House, 1974.

This is an excellent book for comparison. When you have finished an overview of a book, compare your outline to Baxter's.

Baxter, J. Sidlow. *The Strategic Grasp of the Bible: A Series of Studies in the Structural and Dispensational Characteristics of the Bible.* Grand Rapids: Zondervan Publishing House, 1968.

Gray, James M. *Synthetic Bible Studies: Containing an Outline Study of Every Book of the Bible, With Suggestions for Sermons, Addresses, and Bible Expositions. New Edition – Revised and Enlarged.* Old Tappan, New Jersey: Fleming H. Revell Company, 1906.

Kuist, Howard T. *These Words Upon Thy Heart: Scripture and the Christian Response.* Richmond, VA: John Knox Press, 1947.

Lee, Robert. *The Outlined Bible: Each Book in the Bible Introduced, Outlined and Analyzed.* Glasgow, Scotland: Pickering & Inglis Ltd., 1981; reprint, Grand Rapids: Zondervan, 1982.

Morgan, G. Campbell. *The Analyzed Bible.* Old Tappan, New Jersey: Fleming H. Revell Company, 1964.

Morgan, G. Campbell. *Living Messages of the Books of the Bible: Old and New Testaments, One Volume Edition.* Old Tappan, New Jersey: Fleming H. Revell Company, 1962.

Scroggie, William Graham. *Know Your Bible: A Brief Introduction to the Scriptures.* Old Tappan, New Jersey: Fleming H. Revell Company, 1974.

Scroggie, William, Graham. *The Unfolding Drama of Redemption: The Bible as a Whole, Three Volumes in One.* Glasgow, Scotland: Pickering and Inglis, Ltd.; Vol. 1, 1953; Vol. 2, 1957; Vol. 3, 1970; reprint, Grand Rapids: Zondervan Publishing House, 1972.

Books About Learning in General

Adler, Mortimer J., and Charles Van Doren. *How to Read a Book.* New York: Simon and Schuster, 1972.

This is one of the best books, if not the best book I have ever read. It is a treatise on how to learn. Adler is a professor of classic literature and the general editor of *Great Books of the Western World.* Pay particular attention to his chapter on reading sacred books as well as his thoughts on the use of commentaries. Additionally, if you read his introduction to the Great Books in Volume one of that series entitled *The Great Conversation,* you will benefit.

Concordances

Strong, James. *Strong's Exhaustive Concordance.* Crusade Bible Publishers Inc., Unknown.

This is the standard by which all other concordances are judged. The numbering system has become nearly universal in its use. The only drawback to this is its basis on The King James Version.

Wigram, George V. The New Englishman's Hebrew Concordance: Coded to Strong's Concordance Numbering System. Peabody, Massachusetts: Hendrickson Publishers, 1984.

All English concordances, as Strong's, are limited by the fact that they document the usage of English words in a text. The difficulty with this comes from the fact that several Greek or Hebrew words can be translated into the same English word in certain contexts. Wigram solved this by rearranging the concordance to the use of Hebrew words in this work and Greek in the one that follows. This allows the reader to see where a particular Greek or Hebrew word is used in the Bible and allows a tighter cross reference or word study. Strong numbers have been added so the reader does not need to be able to read Hebrew radicals.

Wigram, George V. and Ralph D. Winter. *The Word Study Concordance: A modern, improved, and enlarged version of both The Englishman's Greek Concordance and the New Englishman's Greek Concordance.* Wheaton, Illinois: Tyndale House Publishers, Inc., 1978.

This book and its companion *The Word Study New Testament* is an extension of Wigram's work. The addition of the interlined Strong numbers in the New Testament made the use of the tool very effective.

Young, Robert, LL. D. D. *Analytical Concordance to the Bible.* Grand Rapids: Wm. B. Eerdmans Publishing Company, 1972.

Dictionaries and Lexicons

Bauer, Walter. *A Greek – English Lexicon of the New Testament and Other Early Christian Literature.* 4th Edition. Translated by William F. Arndt and F. Wilber Gingrich. Chicago: The University of Chicago Press, 1957.

This is the standard Greek Lexicon, it is usually referred to as BAG for Bauer, Arndt, and Gingrich. My copy does not have Strong numbers, but I understand that it is available with Strong numbers now. If you do not have the numbers, you have to know enough Greek to get from the passage you are looking at to the root word in BAG.

Brown, Colin, ed. *The New International Dictionary of New Testament Theology.* In three volumes. Grand Rapids: Zondervan Publishing House, 1976; fourth printing, 1979.

This is called a poor man's Kittle. It is a more recent work and much less expensive than the work that follows.

Kittle, Gerhard, ed. *Theological Dictionary of the New Testament.* In ten volumes. Translated by Geoffrey W. Bromiley, D. LITT., D.D. Grand Rapids: Wm. B. Eerdmans Publishing Company, 1964; reprint, 1983.

This is the standard word study. It is exhaustive. It is German in origin, and therefore, cannot be used uncritically. This work takes each word studied and does diachronic, through time, and synchronic, in time, examinations of the usage of the words. It's simply the best.

The Analytical Greek Lexicon: Consisting of An Alphabetical Arrangement of Every Occurring Inflection of Every Word Contained in the Greek New Testament Scriptures, With a

Grammatical Analysis of Each Word, and Lexicograpical Illustration of the Meanings. A Complete Series of Paradigms, with Grammatical Remarks and Explanations. Grand Rapids: Zondervan Publishing House, 1970; 12th Printing, 1975.

If one does not know Greek, this will allow you to get from a Greek text to the root and know what form of the word is being used. One can then go to a Greek grammar and learn more about that type of usage in the New Testament.

Vine, W. E., M.A. *An Expository Dictionary of New Testament Words with their Precise Meanings for English Readers.* Old Tappan, New Jersey: Fleming H. Revell Company, 1966.

This is a good dictionary. It is not of the scope of Brown or Kittle, but has many great insights into the use of some of the more common Greek words.

Word Studies

Bengel, John Albert. *New Testament Word Studies.* In Two Volumes. Grand Rapids: Kregel Publications, 1971.

This is a reprint of an old text and is very good.

Girdlestone, Robert B., M.A. *Synonyms of the Old Testament: Their Bearing on Christian Doctrine.* Grand Rapids: Wm. B. Eerdmans Publishing Company, 1976.

In word studies it is sometimes helpful to understand which words are synonyms of the word you are studying. This can give insight into the work you are doing.

Harris, R. Laird, Gleason L. Archer, Jr., and Bruce K. Waltke. *Theological Wordbook of the Old Testament.* In two volumes. Chicago: Moody Press, 1980.

This work is similar in concept if not scope to Kittle and Brown for Hebrew. It uses Strong numbers to identify and index each word so one can navigate the Hebrew.

Robertson, A.T. *Word Pictures in the New Testament.* Oak Harbor: Logos Research Systems, 1997.

Excellent work for non-Greek students, by a renowned Greek scholar. My copy is electronic. It is still available in print and well worth the investment.

Trench, Richard C., D.D. *Synonyms of the New Testament: Studies in the Greek New Testament.* Grand Rapids: Wm. B. Eerdmans Publishing Company, 1976.

See comment on Girdlestone.

Vincent, M. R. *Word Studies in the New Testament.* McDill AFB, FL:MacDonald Publishing Company, Unknown.

If you can find this, it is a good resource. It is an examination of the usages of words in context.

Wuest, Kenneth S. *Wuest's Word Studies From the Greek New Testament For The English Reader.* In three volumes. Grand Rapids: Wm. B. Eerdmans Publishing Company, 1973.

This is a great study. Wuest looks at the use of words in the specific context of a book. He does not always look at the word that you may be studying, but when he does, it is a good resource.

Greek Language

Dana, H. E., Th.D. and Julius R. Mantey, Th.D., D.D. *A Manual Grammar of the Greek New Testament.* New York: MacMillan Publishing Co., Inc., 1955; reprinted, 1957.

This is the standard grammar for most courses. It is fairly easy to navigate.

Han, Nathan E. *A Parsing Guide to the Greek New Testament.* With and introduction by Merrill C. Tenney. Scottsdale, Pennsylvania/Kitchener, Ontario: Herald Press, 1971.

This is like the analytical lexicon mentioned above except that it is arranged in New Testament book order and parses each verb in each verse, making it quicker to use. Note it contains verbs only, so for nouns you would still need the analytical lexicon.

CPSIA information can be obtained at www.ICGtesting.com
Printed in the USA
LVOW031016230911

247552LV00004B/1/P